QSE

QUICK SMART ENGLISH

Intermediate
B1-B2

Ken Wilson

and

Mary Tomalin

BROOKEMEAD ENGLISH
LANGUAGE TEACHING

Intermediate

Series editor: Duncan Prowse
Contributor: Cheryl Pelteret
Consultant: Rosemary Harris
Assistant editor: Anna Kutz
Designer: John Anastasio
Research and permissions: Veena Holkar,
                                    Pupak Navabpour
Illustrators: Cedric Knight, Mark Duffin
Glossary: Mary Rigby
Recordings: John Green, Tim Woolf

QSE Intermediate
Common European Framework Level B1-B2
Revised for Cambridge ESOL FCE 2008+ and
Trinity College, London GESE and ISE 2007 – 2010

Student's book
ISBN: 978-1-905248-04-9

Also available:
QSE Intermediate
Workbook, ISBN 978-1-905248-05-6
Audio CD 1 Listening + Unit 0, ISBN 978-1-905248-24-7
Audio CD 2 Reading, ISBN 978-1-905248-07-0
Teacher's Guide, ISBN 978-1-905248-19-3

Other books in the QSE Series:
QSE Pre-Intermediate (CEFR A2-B1)
QSE Advanced (CEFR B2-C1)

Produced and published by:
Brookemead English Language Teaching, London

www.brookemead-elt.co.uk

Acknowledgements

Cover: top: Digital Vision/Getty Images; middle left: Photofusion Picture Library/Alamy; middle: Inmagine; bottom: © dickeyphoto.com.
Unit 1: p8tl: Jason Jones; p8tr: © Henry Diltz/CORBIS; p8ml: Dennis MacDonald/Alamy; p9t: Image Source/Alamy; p9m: imageshop - zefa visual media uk ltd/Alamy; p9b:BananaStock/Alamy; p10: Photofusion Picture Library/Alamy; p11t: Solomon Asch Center. **Unit 2:** p12t: © Craig Tuttle/CORBIS; p12b: Rick Gerharter 2003; p13tr: © nagelestock.com/Alamy; p13bl: AP/Wide World Photos; p14:AP/Wide World Photos.
Unit 3: p16l: Empics/AP; p16m: Empics / PA; p16r: Jayne Fincher, Photo Int/Alamy; p17t: POPPERFOTO/Alamy; p17m: Empics/AP, p17b: Empics/Abaca; p18l: Fotoman/Alamy; p18r: Everynight Images/Alamy; p19tm: Paul J. Richards/Getty Images; p19tr:Shaun Heasley/Getty Images. **Unit 4:** p20ml, br: Steve Bloom Images/Alamy; p20mr: Images Etc/Alamy; p20bl: RubberBall/Alamy; p21tl: © New England Aquarium, p21tr: Photo © Scotch Macaskill; p21b: © Brooke McDonald/Sea Shepherd, p22:© PETA, www.peta.org, p23: © Phillip and Baiju McCubbins.
Unit 5: p24tl: Nana Varveropoulou; p24tr: Inmagine, p24m:Janine Wiedel Photolibrary/Alamy, p25t:Courtesy of The Illustrated London News Picture Library, p25b: *Women's Slave Narratives*, Annie L. Burton, Dover Publishing; p26tr:Don Brownlow/Alamy; p26br:Topfoto/HIP; p27br: Mary Evans Picture Library. **Unit 6:** p28tl: Alex Segre/Alamy; p28tr: Brand X Pictures/Alamy; p28ml: Duncan Prowse; p29:© Poseidon/Vision IQ; p30l: Zeraxis Limited, www.zeraxis.com Tel: 44-(0)870-750-6680 Global RFID implementation and systems integration services; p30m:© Gabe Palmer/CORBIS; p30r: Stock Connection/Alamy. **Unit 7:** p32tl:Bryan and Cherry Alexander Photography; p32tr:photographer Randy Montoya, Sandia National Laboratories; p32mr:DOE/NREL - photographer Alan Ford; p33:UCLA Henry Samueli School of Engineering and Applied Science; p34:Professor Kamaruzzaman Sopian. **Ext Read 1:** p36t p37 TEXT: from *Captain Corelli's Mandolin* by Louis de Bernières, published by Vintage (May 1995). Reprinted by permission of The Random House Group Ltd.; p37t: Moviestore Collection. **Unit 8:** p38tr:Sally and Richard Greenhill/Alamy; p38m:Jeff Greenberg/Alamy, p38mr:Jackson Smith/Alamy; p39l:SuperStock/Alamy; p39r:Steve Skjold/Alamy; p40:Inmagine/Alamy; p41l: ImageState/Alamy; p41r:Network Photographers / Alamy. **Unit 9:** p42t:Don Tremain/Alamy; p42m:Adopt-A-Minefield / www.landmines.org; p42b:U.S.Navy imagery used in illustration without endorsement expressed or implied; p43:REUTERS/Kevin Coombs, p43TEXT:© NICK PATON WALSH 2003/The Guardian; p44l:Sipa Press/Rex Features, p44r:REUTERS/Alessia Pierdomenico, p46:UN/DPI Photo.
Unit 10: p46tr: Topfoto/ ImageWorks; p46m:Michael Dwyer/Alamy, p46mr:ImageState/Alamy, p46br:Black Star/Alamy, p47tr:Wern Fawr Manor Farm, p47bl:A family portrait by Luke Martineau 2001, p48:TopFoto/HIP, p49tl:Janine Wiedel Photolibrary/Alamy. **Unit 11:** p50tl:Richard Levine/Alamy; p50m:A1PIX; p51l:Design Pics Inc./Alamy; p51r:A1PIX; p51TEXT:USA TODAY, July 2, 2002. Reprinted with Permission; p52:SuperStock/Alamy. **Unit 12:** p54tm:Allianz Arena/B. Ducke; p54tr:© Don Barker (www.binglebongle.com); p54m:Copyright Matt Lepkowski 2003, Courtesy of TravelsInParadise.com; p55ml: Tom Arnold Images/Alamy; p56tl:© Transrapid International GmbH &Co. KG; p56mr:Gaumont-British (The Kobal Collection); p57tl:Louis Held (Photographie) Portrait Walter Gropius um 1922-1923 Silver gelatine print; p57ml:Getty Images. **Unit 13:** p58tl:© SanWild Trust. For further information please visit: www.bloodybusiness.com and www.sanwild.org; p58tr:copyright Robert Semeniuk; p59:EMPICS/AP, p60tl, tm:Tony Waltham/ Geophotos, p60tr:© Donna Hruska, 2005. All Rights Reserved; p61tl: Source: US National Archives; p61mr:Public Domain/Columbine High School. **Ext Read 2:** p62:Copyright Guardian Newspapers Limited 1998, p63:© Jeroen Bouman/Panos Pictures, p63TEXT:Copyright Guardian Newspapers Ltd 2004. **Unit 14:** p64tr:© LUCASFILM/20TH CENTURY FOX/THE KOBAL COLLECTION; p64m:Bloomsbury; p64mr: © Ambassadors Theatre Group; p65tr: © 2002 L L Prindle, Excerpt from A WIZARD OF EARTHSEA by Ursula K. Le Guin. Copyright © 1968, 1996 by the Inter-Vivos Trust for the Le Guin Children. Reprinted by permission of Houghton Mifflin company. All rights reserved; p66l: © Warner Brothers, p66r:© PARAMOUNT / THE KOBAL COLLECTION / BOLAND, JASIN, p67:© UNIVERSAL/THE KOBAL COLLECTION. **Unit 15:** p68tl:A1PIX, p68tr:Bubbles/John Powell; p68bl:Transtock Inc./Alamy; p68br:A1PIX, p69: Comstock Images/Alamy; p70r:photographer Holly Vogel, taken from HMI World article July/August 2002, p71:Source: National Statistics website:http://www.statistics.gov.uk/CCI/nugget.asp?ID=11&Pos=2&ColRank=2&Rank=448: Crown copyright material is reproduced with the permission of the Controller HMSO. **Unit 16:** p72tl:James Underwood/Alamy, p72ml: Shout/Alamy, p72mr: Michael Dwyer/Alamy, p73tr: David Crausby/Alamy, p73m:AFP/Getty, p74:Empics/AP Images, p75tr:© William T. Ayton is a British artist residing in the Hudson Valley in upstate New York. His work deals with mythologies, the human condition and social themes. More of his work can be seen at www.ayton.net.
P75m:UN/DPI Photo. **Unit 17:** p76tr:© dickeyphoto.com, p76m:Stock Connection/Alamy; p76mr:SuperStock/Alamy, p77: © 2004. Aron Ralston. All rights reserved, p77 TEXT:Cliff Ransom/National Geographic Image Collection; p78l:Picture Scottish Viewpoint; p78r:Reproduced by permission of Ordnance Survey on behalf of HMSO. © Crown copyright 2005. All rights reserved. Ordnance Survey licence number 100044486; p79tl:Mireille Vautier/Alamy. **Unit 18:** p80t:ImageState/Alamy; p80m,b:NASA Jet Propulsion Laboratory (NASA-JPL); p81tm:NASA/ CXC/SAO; p81tr:Chuck Pefley/Alamy, p82l,r,p83:NASA Jet Propulsion Laboratory (NASA-JPL). **Ext Read 3:** p85: © Bettmann/CORBIS, p85TEXT:© 1942 The Estate of Beryl Markham. With Permission of the Proprietor and Pollinger Ltd.

Every effort has been made to trace and acknowledge the copyright holders of all material used in this book.
The publishers apologise for any omissions and will be pleased to make necessary arrangements when this book is reprinted.

QSE Intermediate

CONTENTS

Quick Smart English Intermediate CONTENTS

1 *The BIG question:* ARE YOU A 'GOOD' SHOPPER?

FACT: Over the past decade, Britain has lost nearly 30,000 independent food and drink shops – more than 40% of the total.

2 PREVIEW

Words:

A Where in your neighbourhood can you buy the items in the photographs?
1 at a hypermarket?
2 in a supermarket?
3 in small, local shops?
4 at a farmers' market?

B Which of the items in the photos are:
1 manufactured products?
2 agricultural produce?

(a) mountain bike

(d) dairy produce

(c) vegetables

(b) washing powder

(e) laptop computer

C Match the category with the example.

Category	Example
1 farm crops	(a) beef
2 dairy produce	(b) coal
3 textiles	(c) cheese
4 manufactured products	(d) tuna
5 minerals	(e) clothes
6 meat	(f) souvenirs
7 timber	(g) cars
8 fish	(h) furniture
9 tourism	(i) wheat

- If you want to know exactly what's in your food, then you **should** buy local produce.
- If you want cheap, delicious food, **try** the weekly farmer's market.

D Which words give advice or say that something is a good idea?

E Does **due to** mean the same as **because of**?

SEE WORKBOOK UNIT 0

Language: Read the sentences and answer the questions.
- Everyone wears global brands.
- Global brands are worn by everyone.
- Local farmers produce all our food.

A Do the first two sentences have the same meaning?

B What is the subject of each sentence?

C Rewrite the third sentence without changing the meaning. Begin: *All our food* …..

- **Because of** the children and my job, I never have much time.
- **Due to** global warming, it won't be long before mangoes are grown here.

Ideas: The following sentences are from the reading text on the opposite page. Read them and answer the questions.
- The advantage is (that) it sells everything and it's cheap.
- Supermarket food often travels long distances and that is very bad for the environment.
- It's a disadvantage (that) some of the local shops have closed.

A What kind of shop does the first sentence refer to? What kind of things can you buy there?

B Are the statements in the second sentence true? If so, why?

C Are local shops closing in your neighbourhood? If so, why?

3 READING 🔊 19

A Scan texts 1-5 quickly. Complete the gaps with the type of shop each person is talking about.
(a) hypermarket (b) supermarket (c) local shops

1 *Mike*

Everyone in my family is really busy, and my mum often gets take-away food. We also drive to the .... and shop there. The advantage is that it sells everything and it's cheap. I bought my iPod there and the latest PlayStation game – but I buy my DVDs online. I want a new computer – the .... has some really cheap ones at the moment. My dad says they're made in China and that's due to globalisation – but I'm **not bothered**!

2 *Giorgio*

I'm a chef in a restaurant. All our food is produced by local farmers. If you want to know exactly what's in your food, then you should buy local or **regional produce**. Supermarket food often travels long distances by road or air and that is very bad for the environment. Because of this, we buy our food from .... and farmers. Due to global warming, it won't be long before mangoes are grown around here!

3 *Samantha*

I'm a fashion student and I don't want to buy global brands – they're worn by everyone and that's boring. I'd love to wear **designer** clothes but I can't afford them. Besides, everyone should create their own style. My friends and I buy second-hand clothes in .... or T-shirts and dresses in the street market. We mix colours and styles to make our own individual looks. The advantage is that we save money and help the environment.

4 *Rachel*

Because of the children and my job, I never have much time. Luckily, we have a .... nearby, where I can do my weekly shopping. I also **shop online**. It's a disadvantage that some of the local shops have closed since the .... arrived a few years ago. But I don't mind if the meat is imported from Brazil or the vegetables are grown in Africa – time is the most important thing for me.

5 *Helena*

A lot of tourists come here in summer and want to buy souvenirs of the region. We produce everything locally - the honey, the pottery, textiles and **leather goods**. This region is famous for its ceramics so we sell a lot of mugs, vases and plates. As a local shopkeeper, I buy most things in the .... The disadvantage is the cost - they're often more expensive than the supermarket. But if you want delicious local produce, try the weekly farmers' market – it's great!

B Answer the questions using one of the words or phrases **in bold** in the texts.
1 What is a handbag an example of?
2 How can you shop without leaving home?
3 What do we call someone who makes fashionable, expensive clothes?
4 What phrase can we use when we don't care about something?
5 What do we call fruit and vegetables produced in a certain part of the country?

C Complete the sentences:
1 iPods .... cheaply in the hypermarket.
2 Samantha helps the environment when she buys ....
3 Giorgio thinks mangoes will soon grow in his region because of ....
4 Helena sells mugs and vases because they .... locally.

D 1 Underline the sentences in texts 1-5 that refer to advantages and disadvantages.
2 Why do some of the people prefer to use local shops and markets?
3 Why do others prefer to go to supermarkets or hypermarkets?

4 TALK ABOUT IT

A Work in groups. Talk about how and where you buy things. Use **Language Bank 0** to help you explain the advantages and disadvantages to each other.

B Work in pairs. Imagine that a friend has just moved to your neighbourhood. Talk about where to shop.

C Some people are angry about supermarkets and hypermarkets. Can you explain why?

5 LISTEN IN

A What are the objects in the photos 1-6 made out of? Choose from these materials:

(a) newspaper (b) glass bottles (c) Coke cans
(d) textiles (e) car tyres (f) plastic bags

Now make sentences:
- Example: I think the (hat) is made out of (newspaper).

B You will hear Ruth and Neil Thomson talk about their exhibition called "kNOwtrash". The exhibition has four parts. Listen and complete the gaps with numbers 1-4.
(a) Part .... gives advice about recycling.
(b) Part .... shows things that come out of the ground.
(c) Part .... shows that in nature there is no waste.
(d) In Part .... , all the products are made out of recycled materials.

C Complete the sentences with one or two words.
1 The handbag with the Brazilian flag on it is made out of ....
2 Ruth and Neil say, "There's no .... if you .... trash."
3 Neil says that in nature, ... is recycled.
4 When we manufacture things, we use a lot of ....
5 In the West, we .... a lot of things and do not recycle them.
6 Ruth says that a drinks can is ....
7 In Part 3, Neil shows a Brazilian handbag, a .... , a .... and some ....
8 The recycled objects in Part 3 are made by people in ....
9 Neil says that if you want to help the environment, you should ....
10 He says that another advantage is that you can make .... from recycling.

D Write sentences using the present simple passive tense. Put the verb into the correct form.
1 The toy aeroplane / make out of / drinks cans
2 In nature / nothing / waste
3 In the West, products / use / short time
4 A lot of rubbish / throw away

E Work in small groups. Which of the items below are thrown away in your neighbourhood? Which are recycled? How do you feel about recycling? Explain why.

waste food	drinks cans	plastic bags
glass bottles	old clothes	car tyres
paper / newspaper	plastic bottles	furniture

The Eden Project is an environmental theme park in south-west England.

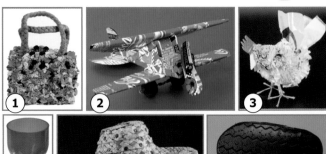

6 CONTROVERSY

Work in pairs. Student A's family have a garden and grow their own vegetables. Student B lives in an apartment with no garden. Discuss the advantages and disadvantages of growing your own vegetables.

SEE ROLE CARDS FOR UNIT 0

7 PORTFOLIO WRITING

Imagine that you are a journalist. Write a review (170 - 200) words the "kNOwtrash" exhibition.

Introduction:	Say where the exhibition is and briefly describe it. *This exhibition is all about rubbish! It shows* .....
Paragraphs 2 & 3:	Describe each part of the exhibition. *The first part shows* .....
Last paragraph:	Give your opinion of the exhibition. *I really enjoyed seeing the exhibition and I learnt a lot.*

8 ECONOMICS in English

A Before you read the text, answer these questions.
  1 What is the difference between a developed and a developing country?
  2 Which countries' economies have grown a lot in recent years?

The BRIC economies

The world economy is changing rapidly. Four developing countries, Brazil, Russia, India and China, which together are called the BRIC economies, are growing especially fast. It is predicted that by 2050 China's economy may be bigger than Japan's or even America's and the BRIC countries will have 40% of the world's population. Experts say that the BRIC economies will be bigger than the economies of today's six largest developed nations, USA, Japan, Germany, Britain, France and Italy. Unfortunately, rapid economic growth causes a lot of pollution.

(a) trees   (b) oil   (c) computers   (d) beef cattle   (e) films   (f) gas   (g) pollution   (h) textiles

B Read the text and answer the questions.
  1 Which countries are known as the BRIC economies?
  2 Which country may have the world's largest economy by 2050?
  3 Which six countries have the biggest economies today?

C Look at the map showing the BRIC countries. Match the pictures with countries and use the verbs in the box below to make passive sentences.

• Example: *Coffee is grown in Brazil.*
1 .... make + *in*   2 .... manufacture + *in*
3 .... produce + *in*   4 .... find + *in*
5 .... raise + *in*   6 ...... cut down + *in*
7 .... export + *from*   8 .... create + *in* ....

9 YOUR TOPIC

A Work in pairs. Make a list of about four products or types of produce from one of these categories: *national, regional, local*.

B As a class, combine your work to make bigger lists by categories (e.g. *textiles, manufactured goods*) and the places they come from.

C Choose one of the categories and prepare a two-minute presentation about it. Say where items come from and where people can buy them.

10 *Your answer:* ARE YOU A 'GOOD' SHOPPER?

Having read this unit, what do you think? Discuss these questions with the rest of the class. Here are some suggestions to help you with the answers.

A What is a 'good' shopper, in your opinion? Give examples.
• A 'good' shopper tries to help the environment when he / she shops.

B In what ways are you a 'good' shopper?
• I think I am a 'good' shopper. All our food is grown locally.
• I'm not really a 'good' shopper. The disadvantage is that it takes too much time.

C How else do you try to help the environment? If you don't, explain why not.
• I don't use many plastic bags. And I often buy recycled paper.
• Because of my job I travel a lot. I don't care if it causes pollution.

What's new?

Subject:	Relationships
Function:	Giving advice, making suggestions, giving opinions
Grammar:	*should, ought to, could, you'd better*

1 *The BIG question:* IS THE INTERNET A GOOD PLACE TO MEET PEOPLE?

 FACT: Nearly a quarter of Japanese high school students regularly visit online dating websites.

2 PREVIEW

(c)

(a)

(b)

 OPEN TO THE PUBLIC

Words:

A Which of these places are in the photos?

1	a pop music festival	2	a crowded club
3	a private party	4	an art gallery
5	an internet café	6	a college library

B Which of the places in A are good for meeting new people?

C Discuss the difference in meaning between the following words:

1	a relationship	3	a romance
2	a friendship	4	a date

D What do you know about the following?
1 Online dating websites
2 Online personal ads (advertisements)
3 Why online dating is so popular
4 The dangers of meeting people online

Language: Read these sentences and then answer the questions.

- People are telling their friends they **should** try it.
- Your first meetings **ought to** be in public places.
- You **could** meet in a coffee shop or a shopping centre.
- If you are already in a relationship, **you'd better** tell the new person before you meet.

A Which of these sentences give advice?
B Which of these sentences make a suggestion?
C Which of the phrases in **bold** uses the infinitive with *to*?
D Do *should* and *ought to* have the same meaning?
E What is the long form of *you'd better*?
1 you had better   2 you would better

SEE WORKBOOK UNIT 1

Ideas: The following sentences are similar to sentences in the reading text on the opposite page. Read them and answer the questions.
- London girl seeks loving man.
- Before your first meeting, you ought to talk on the phone a lot.
- Busy city people in the US find it hard to meet people.

A Where could you see the first sentence?
B Why is it a good idea to talk on the phone a lot before you meet someone?
C Do you think that it's hard to meet people in the city? What's your experience?

3 READING

A Scan each of the texts quickly. In which text (1, 2 or 3):
1 are readers told to be careful when dating online?
2 are we given an example of someone who found a partner online?
3 do people describe the kind of person they are looking for?

2a *Women seeking men*

Where's that loving feeling? I've done the nightlife of London. I want fun and friendship with someone who feels there is beauty in sharing the road of life together and coming home to a loving mate.

1 After five years in New York, Leeane Davis, a school teacher, still didn't have a partner. "There are no Mr Rights in this city," she says. So she decided to try internet dating. [5] After dates with about ten different men, Leeane met Kerry Hooper, a health-food store manager from the suburbs. Three weeks later they decided to get married. [10]

Davis and Hooper are not unusual. **According to research,** 21% of US internet users have **surfed** a personal website and 13% have **posted** an advertisement. Busy city [15] people find it hard to meet people, and online dating has become an acceptable way to find a partner. A researcher says, "People are telling their friends they should try it – **the** [20] **word is getting around**."

Single people are happy to pay up to $30 a month to join internet services that help them search for the right relationship. As a result, [25] online dating is now one of the few internet businesses making big money. It is thought that the US market for online personal ads will rise to more than $600 million [30] by 2007. The same thing is happening in Europe, though more slowly. The internet dating market in the UK [35] **is likely to** grow to £14m in the next four years.

2b *Men seeking women*

Strong hands seek a hold on life: I work very hard, but want to spend time with an independent girl who's passionate and really knows herself. I'm often quiet, but there's a lot under the surface.

2c **Men seeking women**

Crazy for you: I have pulled cats out of trees for old ladies, and there's a picture that looks like me in the National Art Gallery. OK, maybe those things aren't true! I'm looking for adventure. I HATE hot weather. I LOVE cool nights out with a special person.

3 **Trying online dating for the first time? Here's some advice.**
- Keep your identity a secret, but be honest about yourself.
- If you are already in a relationship, you'd better tell the new person before you meet!
- You should find out as much as you can about the other person before you agree to meet. Don't be in a hurry to meet.
- Your first meetings ought to be in public places. For example, you could meet in a coffee shop, or a shopping centre.

B Read Text 1 carefully.
1 Match the words in **bold** in the text with these phrases:
(a) will probably
(b) placed
(c) looked at
(d) more and more people are learning about it
(e) a study of the facts tells us that …..

2 Here is a list of answers. What are the questions?
(a) Ten   (b) 21%   (c) $30   (d) $600 million

C Read the online personal advertisements in Texts 2a, 2b and 2c. Which person:
1 sounds the most amusing?
2 sounds the most romantic?
3 wants to meet someone who has strong feelings?

D Read Text 3. Which piece of advice is most important in your opinion? Explain why.

4 TALK ABOUT IT

Use **Language Bank 1** to help you.
A Work in pairs. Take turns to ask for and give advice about things you should or shouldn't do when you meet someone through online dating.

B Share any stories you have heard about internet dating. Don't talk about your own experiences, or about anyone else in the class. If you talk about the experiences of someone you know, don't say their real name. Or you could make up a story about meeting friends online.

5   LISTEN IN

A Work in pairs. Describe your ideal partner. Here are some words and phrases to help you:

| attractive | (physically) fit | good-looking | a good sense of humour |
| sensitive | intelligent | hardworking | the same ideas | considerate |

B Listen to the conversation and answer the questions.
1   What is Michelle's problem?
2   Can you describe three problems that Michelle says single men have?

C Listen again. The following sentences are slightly different from what the two people said. How are they different? Do the new sentences change the meaning?
1   Do you have a picture of Mr Right?
2   In fact, I think he sounds rather nice.
3   But the really nice guys are all married.
4   They get light in their eyes.
5   Or if they're really attractive, you can be sure they're going out with someone already.

D Work in pairs. Act out a conversation in which a friend gives advice and suggestions to Michelle about how to meet more people. Use **Language Bank 1** to help you. Start like this:
Michelle: • How can I meet more people?
Friend: • I think you ought to join a club.
               Or how about taking up a sport?
               That's a good way to meet people.

E Work in small groups. Discuss this question:
Do you think Michelle is being fair to men? Say why/why not.
Example: • I think it's Michelle who has the problem. She sounds horrible!

F Work in small groups. Discuss the following questions. Use **Language Bank 2** to help you give your opinion.
1   In your country, do many people live together before they get married? Is this a good thing in your opinion?
2   Do you and your friends still think it is important to get married?
3   Do you think people should marry earlier or later? Give reasons for your opinion.
4   What is your opinion of arranged marriages?

6   CONTROVERSY

Work in pairs. Student A wants to find a new partner. Student B gives him or her advice about internet dating. Act out your conversation for the class.

 SEE ROLE CARDS FOR UNIT 1

7   PORTFOLIO WRITING

Work in groups of four or five to prepare a survey on students' dating habits.

Make up a questionnaire of about ten questions. Each member of the group asks four or five other people to answer the questionnaire. When you have their answers, write a factual report on the survey, using the outline below (170 - 200 words).

	Survey Report
Introduction:	*This is a report on a survey of students' dating habits. A group of us gave a questionnaire to (five) students ...*
Questions asked:	*These were the questions we asked ...*
Results:	*Two out of five say that they meet people online.*
Conclusion:	*It is clear from the survey that most people .....*

8 PSYCHOLOGY *in English*

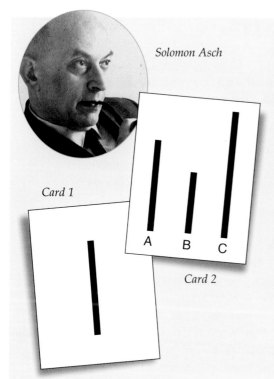

Solomon Asch

Card 1

A B C

Card 2

The Conformity Experiment

In 1958 American **psychologist** (...) Solomon Asch invented an **experiment** (...) to test people's desire **to conform** (...). Groups of students were shown two cards similar to the ones on this page. The students' task was to say which of the three lines on Card 2 (A, B or C) matched the line on Card 1. 5

- In the first **trial** (...), everyone chose the correct line, A.
- In the second trial, again everyone chose correctly.
- Before the third trial, Professor Asch told eight of the nine students, whom he called his **confederates** (...), to choose the wrong line. The **subject** (...), who was the only 10 student who was not a confederate, didn't know this.
- Asch held more trials with many different subjects. In every trial, he told the confederates to choose the incorrect lines.
- The subjects could either say what they saw, or conform 15 to the group's opinion and choose the incorrect line.
- The **results** (...) were astonishing. 76 per cent of the subjects agreed with the incorrect opinion of the **majority** (...) in at least one trial. Overall, the subjects conformed to the incorrect majority in 35 per cent of the trials. 20

A Read the text quickly. Write the number of the definitions below (1–8) in the brackets next to the correct word in **bold** in the text.

1 to behave in the same ways as others in the group
2 people who help someone else do something
3 a scientific test to find out or prove something
4 most of the people or things in a group
5 the information that you get from a scientific experiment
6 a test
7 someone who studies the way people's minds work
8 a person or animal that is used in a test or experiment

B Read the text again.
1 Describe: a) the aim of the experiment
b) the subject's task
c) the subject's problem
d) the results of the experiment
e) the confederates' task

2 Do the results surprise you? Say why/why not.
3 Do you think people need to conform in real life? Can you think of any examples?

9 CONVERSATION

Discuss in pairs. Use **Language Bank 3.**
A How did your parents meet their partners?
B How do you and your friends meet your boyfriends or girlfriends?

10 *Your answer:* IS THE INTERNET A GOOD PLACE TO MEET PEOPLE?

Having read this unit, what do you think? Discuss these questions with the rest of the class. Here are some suggestions to help you with the answers.

A Is internet dating a good way to meet people?
- Yes, but you ought to be careful.
- No, because people aren't always honest about themselves online.

B Do you think you might try online dating?
- I've already tried it! It's great.
- No. There are better ways to meet people.

C How often do you conform to the ideas of the majority?
- Quite a lot. I think it's good to belong to a group.
- I try not to conform too much. I try to be myself.

Unit 2 Bright lights, big city

What's new?

Subject: Country and city life
Function: Comparing and contrasting
Grammar: Comparatives with modifiers

1 *The BIG question:* IS LIFE BETTER IN THE CITY?

FACT: More people live in the cities of China, Brazil and India (such as Shanghai, São Paulo and Mumbai), than in all the cities in the rest of the world.

2 PREVIEW

Words:

A Which of these words would you use to describe the photos?

boring	colourful	exciting	peaceful
suburban	clean	noisy	crowded

Remote countryside in Montana, USA

Street parade in San Francisco

B Complete these sentences. Use a word derived from the word on the left.
  1 boring   I was completely .... with life in my remote village.
  2 noisy   People on mobile phones always talk .... !
  3 exciting   The idea of living in a big city .... me a lot.
  4 colourful   The Gay Pride parade filled the street with ....

Language: Complete these sentences:
A Use words from this list to make a comparison. The arrow indicates if it is more ▲, or less ▼.

expensive	hot	angry	exotic	hectic

Example: ▲ Mumbai is a lot hotter / more exotic than London.

1 ▼ The apartment in Hoboken was far .... than the one in Manhattan.
2 ▲ After an hour and a half, the train was a lot .... than when the power cut started.
3 ▲ The passengers were in a bad mood and became even .... when no one came to help them.
4 ▼ Street life in other cities is much .... than street life in San Francisco.
5 ▼ Suburban life is not .... as life in the centre of New York.

 SEE WORKBOOK UNIT 2

Ideas: The following sentences are from the reading texts on the opposite page. Read the sentences and answer the questions.

● Freedom sips cappuccino in a sidewalk café in San Francisco.
● Nothing but peaceful fields of corn and cows for miles around.
● My clothes are ruined. Now I remember why I left the city in the first place.

A What is the writer saying about San Francisco? Where do you think people feel freer - in the country or in the city? Can you explain why?
B Do you think the second sentence is a good description of life in the country? In your opinion, is the country a lot more boring than the city? Or, do you like the peace and quiet of the countryside?
C What do you imagine was the cause of the problem in the last sentence?

3 READING

A Scan each text and complete the headlines with *love* or *hate*.

1

(a) "Money lives in New York. Power sits in Washington. Freedom sips cappuccino in a sidewalk café in San Francisco." **Joe Flower, American writer about the future**

(b) "People smiled, friendly-like, and we knew we could live here … Los Angeles? That's just a big parking lot where you buy a hamburger for the trip to San Francisco." **John Lennon (1940 –1980), rock singer and Yoko Ono (1933 –), artist**

Why I ___ San Francisco...

(c) "I never saw so many well-dressed, well-fed, business-looking bohemians in my life." **Oscar Wilde (1854 –1900), Irish writer**

(d) "But oh, San Francisco! It is and has everything … The lobsters, clams, crabs. Oh, Cat, what food for you." **Dylan Thomas (1914 – 1953), Welsh poet, in a letter to Cat, his wife**

2

Why I ___ living in New York

Passengers escaping from the New York subway in the blackout

When I was young we went to live in a small town in the Midwest. It was the cleanest, most boring little town you can imagine. Nothing but peaceful fields of corn and cows for miles around. I decided to move to THE CENTER OF THE WORLD. I mean – this is where you get interesting jobs and real money, right? I was really excited 5 when I got a job in an advertising agency in Manhattan – right in the heart of New York.

THERE WAS NO WAY I COULD AFFORD to rent an apartment in Manhattan, but I found a place in Hoboken, New Jersey, which was much less expensive. It was tiny, it was noisy but it was mine, and it was only 45 minutes from the office. I started my new job on August 15th. IT WAS REALLY HECTIC. At 5pm, I walked to the subway, exhausted but excited. I got on 10 the train. There was nowhere to sit down, but I thought – hey, what the hell, this is New York!

Ten minutes later, the train stopped and the lights went out. There was a loud groan from the passengers. One and a half hours later, we were still there. It was getting hotter and the passengers were getting angrier by the minute. It wasn't just a broken-down train. It was far more serious. The whole city had stopped. Thanks to a massive power cut, THERE WAS A 15 BLACKOUT – no electricity from New York all the way to Canada!

A guard told us to walk down the track and climb up into the street through a manhole. I came out covered in oil. A reporter asked me what it was like. "This is my first day in a new job. I put a lot of effort into looking good and my clothes are ruined," I said, pointing to my red dress, which was now black. It was then that I remembered why we left the city in the first place. 20

B Scan Text 1 and choose the more likely meaning for each of the following:
1 Lobsters: (a) sea creatures   (b) snakes
2 Bohemian: (a) a rich business person
                      (b) an artist or writer
3 Parking lot: (a) a place to leave cars
                      (b) a green space in a city

C Read Text 1 again. Highlight one key word about San Francisco from each quotation.

D Read Text 2. Look at the phrases in capital letters and decide which of these things they describe:
1 New York   2 the result of a power cut
3 the cost of city accommodation   4 city life

4 TALK ABOUT IT

Use **Language Bank 4** to give your opinions on these questions:
A What are the strongest images from the two texts?
B Does New York sound like a better place to live than San Francisco? Say why, or why not.
C How does city life compare with life in the country?

5   LISTEN IN

A Look up the definitions of these expressions in your dictionary.

economic migrant   ethnic minority
multi-cultural society   political refugee

B Look at the photo on this page and discuss these questions.

1   Are there any ethnic minorities in your country? If so, have they arrived recently or have they lived there for a long time? How are they treated?

2   What are your feelings about migration? Do you think it should be easier or more difficult to move from one country to another?

New York – a city of many ethnic groups

C You are going to hear interviews with three people about their views on immigration. Listen to the interviews and tick the correct box.

The people	for immigration	against immigration	mixed opinions
Sarah			
Craig			
Mike			

D What did the three interviewees say about these things?

1   Sarah: (a) multi-cultural society   (b) political refugees   (c) jobs
2   Craig: (a) political refugees   (b) a better life   (c) ethnic minorities
3   Mike: (a) jobs   (b) houses   (c) schools

E Read the following sentences. One or two words are different from those in the audio recording. These change the original meaning. Which words are different? How do they change the meaning?

1   We should help people who are a danger to their own countries.
2   Ethnic minorities often live in their own countries.
3   I can see you feel quite wrongly about the subject.

6   CONTROVERSY

Work in threes. Student A, a refugee, accidentally spills coffee over Student B. Student B, who doesn't like immigrants, is rude to him. Student C tries to stop the argument.

SEE ROLE CARDS FOR UNIT 2

7   PORTFOLIO WRITING

Imagine that you are an immigrant in another country. You come from a big house in a village. Now you live in a small apartment in a city. Write an email home (about 120 - 150 words).

Ways to begin: *Hi guys!   Dear (Chuma)*

Useful phrases: *It's much hotter / colder here than at home. I miss the family more and more. People are / aren't as friendly as they are at home. But there's a lot more to do and see.*

Ways to end: *Bye! Take care.*

HUMAN GEOGRAPHY *in English*

A Look at the population charts and answer these questions.
1 What is the difference between a city and an urban area?
2 Which of the urban areas are in the developed world, and which are in the developing world?
3 Are you surprised by any of the locations and sizes of these places? Why?

The world's largest cities:	*Population*	*The world's largest urban areas:*	*Population*
1 Mumbai (Bombay), India	12.6 million	1 Tokyo, Japan	31.2 million
2 Buenos Aires, Argentina	11.9 million	2 New York-Philadelphia, USA	30.4 million
3 Moscow, Russia	11.2 million	3 Mexico DF, Mexico	21.5 million
4 Karachi, Pakistan	10.8 million	4 Seoul, South Korea	20.15 million
5 Dilli (Delhi), India	10.4 million	5 São Paulo, Brazil	19.1 million

B Look at the chart below and find phrases that describe:
1 The life of poor people in the country.
2 What rich city people want and what they do.
3 Services that are better in the city than in the country.

KEY:
Push factors = people are pushed out, or encouraged to leave places.
Pull factors = people are pulled towards places, or attracted to them.

Emigration – OUT OF the city

Push factors:
• High cost and shortage of housing in the city.
• Crime, drugs, pollution, overcrowding.
• Congestion, traffic, high cost of transport.
• Social problems in the inner city.
Pull factors:
• Richer people want space and a clean environment so they move to the suburbs or the country.

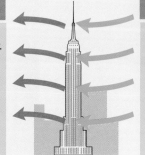

Immigration – INTO the city

Push factors:
• Hard agricultural conditions, poverty in rural areas.
• Poor land, or shortage of land for farming.
• High unemployment.
• Lack of services, such as health care, transport.
Pull factors:
• Better jobs and better pay in the city.
• Better services, such as shops and entertainment.

C Read the text more carefully and answer these questions.
1 Which of the following are Push factors and which are Pull factors? Why?
(a) Shortage of agricultural land   (b) More jobs   (c) Better entertainment   (d) Clean environment
2 Where are these people most likely to live?
(a) The owner of a fashionable shop   (b) A rich, retired business person   (c) A poor artist

9   YOUR TOPIC

Work in groups of four, Pair A and Pair B.
Pair A: Prepare four or five points for a two-minute talk on a topic connected with this unit.
Example: *Why we want to move to another country.*
• Discuss what you want to say and make notes of the main points.
• Make sure you have facts and opinions ready to use in the discussion.
• Begin your talk. Take turns to make points.
Pair B:
• Listen carefully to the points made by Pair A.
• Ask questions and/or ask for clarification of any points you don't understand.

Use **Language Bank 5** to help you.

10   *Your answer:* IS LIFE BETTER IN THE CITY?

Having read this unit, what do you think? Discuss these questions with the rest of the class. Here are some suggestions to help you:
A Is it a problem that so many people want to live in cities?
• Yes, because cities are dirty and crowded.
• No, because there are more jobs in the cities.
B Do you want to live in the city or the country?
• In the city. I think cities are more interesting for young people.
• I would like to live in a city and then move out of the city after a few years.
C Would you like to move to another country?
• Yes – I can get a better job if I do that.
• No – I can have a better life at home.

Fame and fortune

What's new?

Subject:	Public figures and celebrity
Function:	Expressing possibility and uncertainty
Grammar:	*may, might*

1 *The BIG question:* WHAT IS THE PRICE OF FAME?

FACT: A series of robberies at the houses of rich and famous people became known as the *Hello!* Burglaries, because celebrities were robbed after appearing in *Hello!* Magazine.

2 PREVIEW

Words:

A Why are the people in the photographs famous?

1 Nelson Mandela
2 Albert Einstein
3 Bill Gates
4 Nicole Kidman
5 Queen Elizabeth II
6 Tiger Woods

B Discuss these questions with other students.
1 What is a *celebrity*? How do people become celebrities?
2 What are the *media*? How do the media treat celebrities?
3 What is a *stalker*? Why do you think people become stalkers?
4 Are famous people always *talented*?

Language: Read these sentences and then answer the questions.
- Photographers **may** hide because they want a photo of you.
- You **may** not be famous ten years from now.
- The public **may** lose interest in you.
- They **might** even forget all about you.

A Do the words *may* and *might* refer to:
  a) a possible situation?
  b) a situation that will definitely happen?
B Which sentences refer to the future?

C Which sentence talks about something that can happen in a certain situation?

D Write two sentences saying what you may or may not do tomorrow.

E Write two sentences saying what you might do next year.

 SEE WORKBOOK UNIT 3

Ideas: The following sentences are from the reading text on the opposite page. Read them and then answer the questions.
- Fans may decide that they have a 'special relationship' with you. They may stalk you, and climb into your bedroom.
- When you're famous, people say things like, "I think you're wonderful, can I have your autograph?"
- If you're famous, you may have to say goodbye to your privacy.

A Which sentences refer to the disadvantages of fame?
B What are the advantages and disadvantages of fame, in your opinion?
C Why do you think people are so interested in famous people? Why do people want their autographs?
D Have you ever met anyone famous? If so, describe how you met them and what happened?

Fame and fortune

3   READING

A   Scan the article. Which paragraphs are about the plus (+)
and which are about the minus (-) factors of being famous?

SO YOU WANT TO BE FAMOUS?

(a) .... **All the trappings:** Fame can make you very rich. And money can
bring you the high life -- a private plane, a villa in the South of France. Bill Gates'
house near Seattle has only seven bedrooms, but it has 24 bathrooms and six
kitchens, and is worth $97 million.

(b) .... **If it doesn't work out:** Fame gives you the opportunity to fall in love with
famous and attractive partners. Nicole Kidman met Tom Cruise co-starring in the film
Days of Thunder. Within a year, she and Cruise were married. They divorced ten years
later. Fame might not make you happy in the long run!   5

(c) .... **In the limelight:** We all want to be admired. When you're famous, people
say things like, "I think you're wonderful. Can I have your autograph, please?" Famous   10
people may pretend not to like the attention, but in fact, they're secretly pleased.

(d) .... **Power and influence:** Fame may bring you power. If you're famous, you may
have a better chance of getting your opinion heard. If, like Bono from U2, you have Nelson
Mandela's number on your speed-dial (and he has yours), you definitely have influence!

(e) ...... **Public recognition:** Many brilliant people want their achievements to be recognised   15
by the public. It makes them feel their work is worthwhile. Few great achievers are like Albert
Einstein, who said: "My scientific work is motivated by a desire to understand the secrets of
nature -- by nothing else." But he did become world famous and won the Nobel Prize.

(f) .... **Adopt a disguise:** If you're famous, you may have to say goodbye to your privacy.
Photographers may hide near your vacation home, waiting to get a picture of you in your swim   20
suit. You may have to wear a disguise. When the Rolling Stones appeared on television in the
1970s, they went into the studio via the back door -- in trash cans!

(g) .... **Beware of stalkers:** Fans may decide that they have a 'special relationship' with you.
They may stalk you, and climb over your backyard five-metre garden wall and into your bedroom.
The Queen of England and Madonna have both had problems with stalkers.   25

(h) .... **Keeping up appearances:** Once you're famous, you may want to stay famous. But you
have to accept that you may not be a celebrity ten years from now. The public may lose interest in
you. Don't worry! Just enjoy your fame while you have it.

B   Match the phrases above in **bold** (a – h) with these
definitions:

1   Something that you wear so that people will not
recognise you.
2   Pretend everything in your life is wonderful.
3   Luxuries that you can buy if you are rich.
4   Getting a lot of attention from the public and
the media.
5   Having the chance to put your ideas into practice.
6   Watching out for people who take too much
interest in you.
7   Having people know who you are and what
you do.
8   When something does not last as long you
might like.

C   What does the text say about these things or people?

| 1 bathrooms | 2 autographs | 3 Bono |
| 4 Nobel Prize | 5 dustbins | 6 marriage |

D   Read the text carefully.
1   What might a photographer do to get
celebrity photos?
2   What might a stalker do, according to the
writer?
3   What advice does the writer give to famous
people?

4   TALK ABOUT IT

Use **Language Bank 6** to help you.
A   Is there anything in the article you disagree with?
If so, say why.
B   Can you think of other advantages or
disadvantages of fame?
C   Do you know anyone who may become famous?
D   Do you want to become famous?
E   Do you think that the price of fame might be too
high for you?

Fame and fortune

5   LISTEN IN

A Before you listen to an interview with two members of a new band, put these words and expressions into the correct sentences.

(a) album	(b) single	(c) drummer
(d) gig	(e) on tour	(f) come out
(g) in the charts	(h) appear on TV	

1 Can you name the band's ....?
2 Are they going to ....?
3 Is their chart single also on their ....?
4 When did the album ....?
5 Are they doing a .... next Saturday?
6 Does the band have a song .... at the moment?
7 What is the title of their latest ....?
8 Does the band ever go ....?

B Listen to the interview and answer the questions.
1 Why does the audience laugh when Dave speaks?
2 What doesn't Dave know about Sharon?

C Listen again and decide if these sentences are true (**T**) or false (**F**).   **T / F**
1 The band's first single went into the charts at number six. ☐
2 They're writing material for a new single. ☐
3 They are going to Scandinavia and Germany. ☐
4 The new album will come out in the autumn. ☐
5 Sharon has been asked to appear on TV in *The Girl Next Door*. ☐

D Work in pairs. Take turns to talk about your favourite band.
● My favourite band is ...
● Their latest single is ...
● I may see them on tour ...
● I might buy their next album ...

6   CONTROVERSY

Student A is a pop star who does not want to do publicity interviews for a new album because he wants a holiday. Student B is the PR manager who wants the star to appear on TV chat shows.

  SEE ROLE CARDS FOR UNIT 3

7   PORTFOLIO WRITING

Work in pairs to devise and answer a questionnaire to find out people's ideas about fame and celebrity. Write seven questions then give it to another pair to complete.

Example questions:	Example answers:
● Do you think fame changes people?	● Yes, I think fame almost always changes people.
● In what way does it change them?	● It is very difficult for them not to become arrogant.

8 MEDIA STUDIES in English

MAKING NEWS

Are the media simply reporting world events? Do they give us images of famous people and events as they really are? Or do media editors **manage the news** 5 in order to present a **particular point of view**?

In reality editors **select the images** that we see. For example, during the 2003 war in Iraq, 10 American TV news did not show pictures of dead American soldiers, although hundreds of Americans were killed. Was this

US President George W Bush

because the media wanted people 15 to support the war?

The media, which include **Public Relations (PR) managers**, select images and stories that show the

US Senator John Kerry

type of news that they want to 20 present. For example, the photos on this page show that both President George W Bush and Senator John Kerry are strong military leaders. Photographers 25 may use techniques **such as choosing the camera angle** and the location. All these things **influence the message** that the picture has for the viewer. 30

A Look at these photos, taken when the US occupation of Iraq was an important issue for American voters. What images are the photographers trying to present and how is this done?

B Think of two captions for each photo, one that presents the person in a positive way, and one that presents him in a negative way.

C Read the text quickly and check the meanings of the phrases in **bold**.

D Read the text again and answer these questions.
1   How do the media influence the news?
2   Give examples of their methods.

9 INTERACTIVE TASK

Work in groups of four, two pairs in each group. Both pairs prepare a 3–4 minute talk on the same topic, for example, *How The Media Works*. Make a list of four or five main points.

Pair A: Start talking about the topic. Be prepared for Pair B to take control of the conversation. Answer their questions and reply to their comments, for example:	**Pair B:** Listen while Pair A starts the discussion. Let Pair A do most of the talking, but take control of the discussion by asking questions and making comments, for example:
• The media don't show us real news. They show us what they want us to see. • Yes. For example, they set up exactly the images they want to show us.	• Really? That's an interesting idea. Can you explain how they do that? • I think I understand. You mean, they select which images they show?
Use **Language Bank 7** for expressions used to gain time for thought.	

10 *Your answer:* WHAT IS THE PRICE OF FAME?

Having read this unit what do you think? Discuss these questions with the rest of the class. Here are some suggestions to help you:

A Do you want to be famous?
• No. If you are famous, you have no private life.

B Is the price of fame too high for you?
• No it's worth it for all the trappings.
• I'm not sure I would like to be recognised in public.

C Can you be a public figure and remain real?
• Yes, I think it's possible to be rich and real.

1 *The BIG question:* DO ANIMALS HAVE FEELINGS?

FACT: Apart from humans, the ten most intelligent animals are: chimpanzees, gorillas, orang-utans, baboons, gibbons, monkeys, whales, dolphins, elephants, pigs.

2 PREVIEW

Words:

A Underline the names of the animals in both the photos and the FACT box.

B Name ten animals that you think are NOT very intelligent.

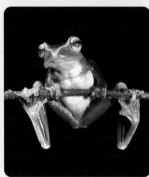

C These words describe feelings or emotions.
Can you think of words which mean the opposite?
Can you think of five more words for emotions?

| joy | grief | love | pleasure | fear |

D 1 When have you felt great joy, grief or fear?
  2 What's the difference between liking someone and loving someone?
  3 Which of the following things gives you most pleasure? (a) good food (b) a good movie (c) a great work of art (d) good friends (e) something else!

Language: Read these sentences and then answer the questions.

- She found a young chimpanzee **that** had starved to death after its mother died.
- There are so many other kinds of food **which** we can eat.
- He's an environmentalist **who** regularly observes whales.
- The scientists **that** I interviewed had studied chimpanzees for many years.

A Can you rewrite each of the sentences above as two sentences?
   Example: • She found a young chimpanzee. It had starved to death after its mother died.

B Which of the words in **bold** refer to things and which refer to people?

C Which of the words in **bold** are the subject of the verb which follows it in the sentence?

D Which of the words in **bold** are the object of the verb which follows?

E Which of the words in **bold** can you omit?

SEE WOOKBOOK UNIT 4

Ideas: The following sentences are from the reading texts on the opposite page. Read them and answer the questions below.

- After mating, the two whales stay by side, stroking each other with their flippers.
- Female sea lions cry loudly when killer whales eat their pups.
- Elephants try to revive family members who are dead or dying, and stand quietly beside them for many days.

A Why do you think the whales behave in this way?

B What emotion are the female sea lions feeling when they cry loudly?

C In what ways does the behaviour of the animals described in the three sentences above remind you of human behaviour?

Animal passions

3 READING ④

A You are going to read three texts about animals and their feelings. Three sentences have been removed from the texts. Choose from the sentences (A)-(D) the one which fits each gap (1)-(3). There is one extra sentence which you do not need to use.

(A) The hunt is an important part of local culture, which dates back 400 years.
(B) There are animals who show no emotions at all.
(C) She says that he died of grief.
(D) Are they in love?

1 Swimming off the coast of Argentina, a female right whale chooses one of the many males who are following her. After mating, the two whales 5 stay side by side, stroking each other with their flippers and finally, roll together in an embrace. The whales then depart, flippers touching, and swim slowly, diving and surfacing 10 together until they disappear from sight. (1) … Biologist Bernd Wrsig is a scientist who regularly observes the amorous right whales near Argentina. 'As a scientist, I should probably say that this event is just an example of a mating strategy. But maybe they behave that way because they're the "right" whales for each other.' Most 15 scientists don't agree with him. 'Whales behave as if they're in love, but you can't prove that they're feeling anything,' says neuroscientist Joseph LeDoux, author of *The Emotional Brain.*

3 Animals feel pleasure – that's certain! Cats purr, dogs wag their tails, even parrots get excited when their owners come into the room. University of Colorado biologist Marc Bekoff says: 5 'Animals at play are symbols of the joy of life. But grief is also common in the wild, particularly following the death of a mate, parent or even close companion. Female sea lions cry loudly when killer 10 whales eat their pups.' Jane Goodall found a young chimpanzee who starved to death after his mother died. (3) … . Kenyan biologist Joyce Poole works with African elephants. She says that they try 15 to revive family members who are dead or dying, and stand quietly beside them for many days. They sometimes reach out and touch the body with their trunks. She says that the behaviour of these animals 20 shows that 'they experience deep emotions and understand about death.'

2 Every year in Japan, hunters trap and kill up to 20,000 dolphins. At Taiji in Central Japan, they force the dolphins into a small inlet, where the water 5 turns red with their blood. (2) … . Izumi Ishii is a local man who used to be a hunter, but now he thinks that the practice should stop. 'It's true that we needed 10 dolphin meat for food in the old days, but now there are so many other things that we can eat. These are intelligent, feeling creatures,' he said. 'They know 15 what is happening and you can see that they feel fear. How is it possible to kill animals that cry and close their eyes at the moment they are killed?' 20

B Read Text 1 and answer these questions:
1 Who chooses the mate – the male or the female right whale? ......
2 Do they spend any time together after mating? ......
3 Can we prove that whales have emotions? ......

C Read Text 2 and decide if the following sentences are true (**T**) or false (**F**). **T/ F**
1 The dolphins are killed in the open sea. ☐
2 Izumi Ishii wants to stop killing dolphins. ☐
3 The dolphins are completely aware of what is happening to them. ☐

D Read Text 3 quickly and find words for:
1 Great sadness ......

2 To die because of not eating ......
3 Part of an elephant's body ......

4 TALK ABOUT IT

Use **Language Bank 8** to help you answer question B.
A Do you think that animals have emotions, like humans? Do they feel sadness or love?
B How do you feel after reading the texts on this page? Try and explain your feelings.
C Do you think that animals play for fun, like humans? Or do they play because this is the way they learn?

This dog is being used to test for skin diseases in a laboratory.

5 LISTEN IN

A Before you listen to a radio debate about animal rights, look at the photo.
  1 Do you agree with vivisection?
  2 Do you think animals like chimpanzees should have the same rights as humans?

B You are going to hear a radio debate between an animal rights activist and a medical research scientist. Before you listen, check the meaning of the following words and expressions.

embarrassment	recognise	prison
sophisticated behaviour	save from extinction
mirror	cruel	resemble	endangered

C Before you listen, which person do you think will have the following opinions? Check your answers after listening.

The opinion	Dr Carla Robinson (Medical research scientist)	Tony Cavell (Animal rights activist)
1 Animals have many of the same feelings that we do.		
2 Zoos are very important. They often save endangered animals from extinction.		
3 Human lives are more important than animal lives.		
4 It's not right to do experiments on primates that are such close relations of humans.		

D After listening, reply to each of the opinions expressed in C with the opposite point of view.

E In the debate you listened to, what are the arguments for and against the following:
  1 The rights of animals such as pigs and rabbits?
  2 The rights of primates?
  3 Keeping animals in zoos?

6 CONTROVERSY

Group A are animal rights activists. Group B are medical research scientists. Debate the rights and wrongs of experiments on live animals.

SEE ROLE CARDS FOR UNIT 4

7 PORTFOLIO WRITING

Write a formal letter to a newspaper, or a minister in your government (120–150 words). Explain why you think we should or shouldn't keep animals in zoos, or use them in experiments.

Begin:	*Dear Editor*
Useful phrases:	*In my opinion, ...*
	I (strongly) believe/feel (that) ....
	I agree with (name) when he/she says ...
	I cannot agree that ...
End: (your name)	*Yours faithfully*

8 ECOLOGY in English

A Read the text below quickly. Write the number of the definitions (1–8) in the brackets next to the correct word in the text.

1 The way in which plants, animals and people are related to each other and their environment.
2 Likely to be harmed, endangered or destroyed.
3 When people or animals try to be more successful than each other.
4 Something that a country, a person, or animal can use.
5 When someone or something continues to live or exist, especially after a dangerous situation.
6 The ecology of a particular area.
7 When all the trees in an area are cut down or destroyed.
8 A substance that carries genetic information in a cell.

Gorilla family in the mountains of Uganda.
In some places they are hunted for bush meat.

1 The more we learn about primates, the more we realise how similar they are to human beings. This is especially true of gorillas, which
5 share 98% of their **DNA** (...) with humans. But sadly, their **survival** (...) is **threatened** (...).
  Gorillas are an important part of the rainforest **ecosystem** (...) of the
10 Ruwenzori Mountains of East Africa. But as the human population in the area increases, farmers are cutting down the rainforest. Timber companies also cause
15 **deforestation** (...), leaving smaller and smaller areas of wilderness. The result is a serious loss of **habitat** (...) for the gorillas. Hunters, who kill the gorillas
20 for bush meat, are another threat.
  How can we balance the ecology of the rainforests, where human beings and gorillas are in **competition** (...) for **resources** (...) within the same
25 environment? One answer is tourism. Foreign tourists pay more than $3 million each year to see three families of protected gorillas in Uganda's National Parks. However, if tourists
30 go too close to the gorillas they can give them human diseases.

B Read the text again. How do the following help or threaten the survival of the gorillas?
1 farmers   2 timber companies   3 hunters   4 tourists   5 national parks   6 diseases

9 CONVERSATION

A Discuss in pairs for about three minutes. Use phrases in this unit and **Language Bank 9** to express agreement or disagreement.
1 Which groups are more important, the gorillas or people who need farms and meat?
2 Do you feel it is important to try and save the gorillas? Explain why.
3 Can we balance the needs of both people and apes within the same environment?

B Explain your feelings about people hunting gorillas for bush meat.
Example answers:
- I think it's horrible. It's really sad that hunters kill primates.
- It upsets me that people are so poor.
- I don't feel upset at all. A gorilla is only an animal.
- It's terrible what we are doing to primates which are similar to human beings.

10 *Your answer:* DO ANIMALS HAVE FEELINGS?

Having read this unit, what do you think? Discuss these questions with the rest of the class. Here are some suggestions to help you with the answers.
A Do animals have feelings like humans?
- Some animals do, for example, chimpanzees.
- I don't believe that animals have real feelings.
B How do you feel about animals?
- I love animals and I hate the idea of vivisection.
- The idea of bush meat makes me feel very upset.
- I've never really been interested in animals.
C Do you think we should do more to protect animals?
- Yes, now that we know that animals have emotions, I think we should.
- Yes, but humans should always come before animals.

What's new?

Subject:	Early memories
Function:	Describing past habits
Grammar:	*used to*; past perfect

1 *The BIG question*: HOW WELL DO WE REMEMBER THINGS?

FACT: Memories are not stored in our brains like books on shelves. When we remember something, we re-make the memory from many words, images and experiences kept in different parts of our brains.

2 PREVIEW

(a)

(c)

(b)

Words:

A 1 What is the difference in meaning between the words in groups a) and b)?

> a) remember   imagine   recall   remind
> b) memory   recollection   imagination   reminder

2 Which word is the odd one out in each list?

B Complete these sentences with one of the words from the lists above.
1 I love this song. It ... me of my holiday in Spain.
2 I have absolutely no ... of meeting him before.
3 I can't ... what it was like to be a slave.
4 She doesn't ... anything about what happened last night.

C Look at the photos and answer the questions.
1 Do you remember anything from your early childhood? If so, what?
2 What do you remember about your first school?
3 Are your most recent memories the strongest? Or are others stronger?

Language: Read the sentences and answer the questions.
- We used to wander from plantation to plantation.
- When she spoke like that, he would get away as quickly as possible.

A 1 Do the sentences refer to something that happened once or many times?
2 Do the sentences refer to things that still happen?
3 Do *used to* and *would* mean the same thing?

- Before we got to the fields, we had eaten nearly all the food.

B 1 Which of the two events in the sentence takes place first?
2 What does the use of *had* + past participle indicate?

SEE WOOKBOOK UNIT 5

Ideas: The following sentences are from the reading text on the opposite page. Read them and answer the questions.

- There was one wooden bowl for fifteen children.
- If the wife had no children in a year or so, she was sold.
- My father owned a plantation about two miles from ours.

A Where do you think the children lived?
B Can you imagine a society where the second event could happen?
C Do you think the writer's father was a stranger?

3 READING

A You are going to read an extract from an autobiography of a slave, with a short introduction. Four sentences have been removed from the text. Choose from the sentences (A)-(E) the one which fits each gap (1)-(4). There is one extra sentence which you do not need to use.

(A) Of course, I followed, and before we got to the fields, we had eaten nearly all the food.

(B) Eventually, Annie moved to Boston, where she wrote her life story.

(C) The younger children went to school instead of working in the fields.

(D) I remember that whenever my mistress spoke like that, he would whip his horse and get away as quickly as possible.

(E) There was no marriage ceremony – the couple jumped over a stick – and they were married.

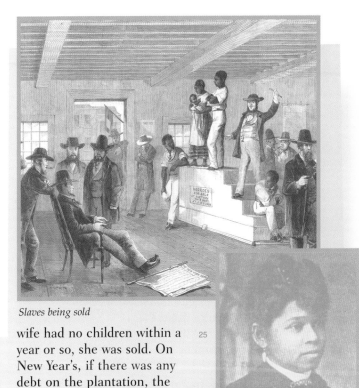

Slaves being sold

Annie L. Burton was born to a slave woman in the 1850s on a plantation in Alabama. Annie's mother was beaten and ran away, but she returned for her children years later after the Civil War, when the slaves were freed.

(1) … . This was published in 1909 as *Recollections of a Happy Life*. This is an extract from the book.

The memory of my happy, carefree childhood days on the plantation, with my little white and black companions, is often with me. We used to wander from plantation to plantation, not knowing or caring what things were going on in the great world outside.

The slaves that were not married used to serve the food from the great house, and about half-past eleven they would send the older children with food to the workers in the fields. (2) … .When the workers returned home, they would complain, and we would be whipped. We children had no supper, and only a little food in the morning. There was one wooden bowl for fifteen children, and oyster shells were our spoons. Sometimes there was bread in our bowl, sometimes greens or bones. Dogs and ducks ate from the bowl as well.

If a slave man and woman wished to marry, a party would be arranged on a Saturday night. (3) … . If the wife had no children within a year or so, she was sold. On New Year's, if there was any debt on the plantation, the extra slaves were sold. Because of this, families were often separated.

My mistress often told me that my father owned a plantation about two miles from ours. He was a white man, born in Liverpool, England. I only saw him a dozen times, when I was about four years old. I saw him only from a distance. Whenever my mistress saw him going by, she would take me by the hand and run after him and exclaim, 'Stop there, I say! Don't you want to see and speak to your darling child? See what a bright and beautiful daughter she is, a perfect picture of yourself!' (4) … . I never spoke to him, and cannot remember that he ever noticed me, or in any way accepted that I was his child.

Annie Burton

B Read the text more carefully and answer the following questions.

1 What does the author mean by the word *mistress*?

2 What happened when the children took food to the workers in the fields?

3 Did the children have enough to eat?

4 Why were slaves sold?

5 Did the author's father visit her?

4 TALK ABOUT IT

Use **Language Bank 10** to help you discuss:

A Why you think Annie Burton called her book *Recollections of a Happy Life*? Was her life really happy?

B Imagine memories like these and describe them in your own words.

- We would be whipped.
- We children had no supper.
- Families were often separated.

C How would you feel if you were a slave like Annie?

D What else do you know about slaves in America and their lives?

Did it really happen?

5 LISTEN IN

A Work in pairs.

1 a) Which of the people in this list might work in a house like the one in the picture?

   b) Which of the people might own or visit a house like this?

| housemaid | lord | film star | chauffeur | cook |

2 What kind of work do you think the servants did? Do you think they enjoyed it?

3 What did visitors to houses like this do?

B You are going to hear an interview with an old lady about her life as a housemaid. Listen and answer the questions.

1 Why did Mary go into domestic service?
2 What were Mary's duties?
3 Did she enjoy her life? Say why.
4 Are you surprised by her answers? If so, why?

Stately home

The servants

C Listen again. Underline the correct answers.

1	Mary started work when she was	a) 20 years old	b) 14 years old
2	Mary worked in	a) two different houses	b) five different houses
3	Mary was paid	a) £18 a year	b) £18 a week
4	Mary had	a) her own bathroom	b) her own bedroom
5	The house was owned by a	a) a film star	b) a lord
6	Mary's husband was	a) a chauffeur	b) the owner of a Rolls Royce

D Read the extract. Cross out the words and expressions that are not necessary for complete understanding.

Julie:	Was it very hard?
Mary:	Er ... well, it depended on the job. I worked in ... oh I can't remember ... in five different houses, I think. They were all, how shall I say? ... great houses – stately homes – that I worked in, with lots of servants.
Julie:	U-huh ... How much were you paid?
Mary:	For my first job, I was paid ... um, let me see, I THINK it was eighteen pounds a year.
Julie:	A YEAR?

6 CONTROVERSY

Work in groups. Student A reads a story, closes the book and whispers the story to Student B, who whispers it to Student C and so on. Does the story change?

 SEE ROLE CARDS FOR UNIT 5

7 PORTFOLIO WRITING

Write a description (170 - 200 words) of some memories of your childhood.

Make notes before you start	• Two brothers; one sister; small house. • Mum worked; Granny often helped.
1 Introduction	• I have many happy memories, but ...
2 Paragraph 1 (basic information)	• My father was away a lot. • I remember that we had a lot of fun.
3 Paragraphs 3 and 4 (stories of childhood)	• I remember falling into the lake. • I don't recall when I learned to swim.
4 Conclusion	• Altogether, it was a happy / sad childhood.

8 HISTORY in English

A Before you read *The Slave Trade*, try to answer these questions.
1   When did the slave trade start?
2   Where did most of the slaves come from?
3   Where did they end up working as slaves?
4   How did slavery in the US end?

B Now read the text and check your answers.

C Are these facts true (**T**) or false (**F**)?   **T/ F**
1   The majority of slaves ended up in the USA.   ☐
2   Traders caught slaves with the help of   ☐
    African chiefs.
3   Many slaves died on the journey across the   ☐
    Atlantic.
4   The British abolished the slave trade in 1833. ☐
5   Slavery in America ended after the Civil   ☐
    War.

9 INTERACTIVE TASK

Work in groups of four, Pair A and Pair B. As a group, choose a topic for a 3 – 4 minute talk for example:
● Being a servant, or Being a slave.
Pair A: Make notes about points you want to make. Start talking about the topic, for example:
● In our house, the servants used to work very hard.
Be prepared for Pair B to take control. Answer their questions and reply to their comments.
Pair B: Take control of the discussion by asking questions and making comments, for example:
● How much were you paid?
● That's not very much. Today servants are paid…
Use **Language Bank 11** to help when you hesitate.

10 *Your answer:* HOW WELL DO WE REMEMBER THINGS?

Having read this unit, what do you think? Is it easy or difficult for you to remember your childhood clearly? Here are some suggestions to help you:
A What are your first memories?
● I remember my first bedroom.
● We used to have a dog.
B Do you remember your first teacher?
● I think her name was Mrs Jones.
● No, actually, Mrs Smith often taught us.
C What are your strongest memories?
● I remember falling into the river.

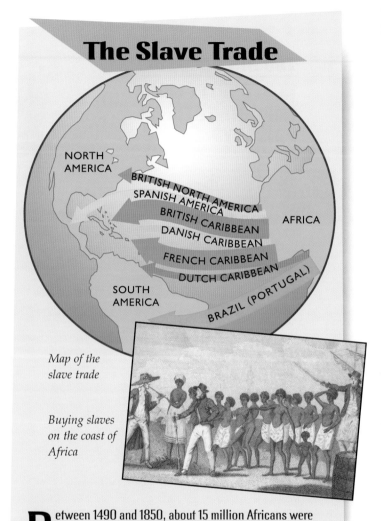

The Slave Trade

Map of the slave trade

Buying slaves on the coast of Africa

Between 1490 and 1850, about 15 million Africans were transported to the Americas as slaves. They were mostly used to work on cotton, sugar and tobacco plantations.
The Portuguese and the British were the main slave traders. Most slaves were taken to the Caribbean islands, Brazil, and Spanish America. Only about six percent were sent to the USA. Slaves were bought from chiefs along the coast of West Africa. Traders paid for them with textiles, brandy, horses and especially guns.   5
Life on the slave-ships was terrible. Crossing the Atlantic Ocean took between 25 and 60 days. Slaves were crowded onto the lower decks only about one and a half metres high, chained together by their hands and feet. Many slaves died on the journey. Some of them killed themselves by refusing to eat. Only half of them were strong enough to work when they arrived.   10

   15

The British abolished the slave trade in 1833, but it continued for many years. In America, the election of Abraham Lincoln as president, and the American Civil War (1861 – 1865), brought an end to slavery in the USA.   20

You are being watched

What's new?

Subject:	Technology
Function:	Describing pictures
Grammar:	Present and past simple passives

1 *The BIG question:*
IS SECURITY MORE IMPORTANT THAN PRIVACY?

FACT: Surveillance cameras can find the face of one person in a crowd of 50,000.

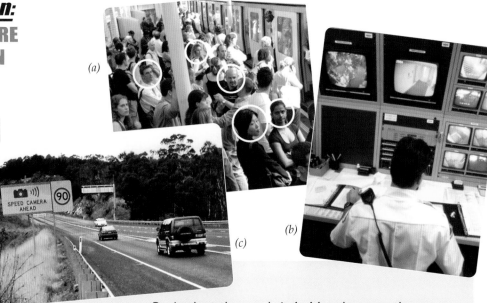

(a)

(b)

(c)

2 PREVIEW

Words:

A Which of these sentences fit which photos?
1. Speed cameras are used to catch people driving too fast.
2. A surveillance camera tracks people in public places.
3. A security officer monitors CCTV images.

B What is your reaction to the FACT above? Use some of these words:

not interested	horrified	surprised
reassured	worried	pleased

C Do you agree with ✓ or disagree with ✗ these statements?
1. Surveillance cameras are an invasion of personal privacy. ☐
2. CCTV makes public places such as shopping malls safer. ☐

Language:

A Read these sentences and answer the questions.
- Each day, speed cameras photograph thousands of drivers.
- Each day, thousands of drivers are photographed by speed cameras.
  1. Do these sentences mean the same?
  2. What is the subject of each sentence?
  3. Which are the most important words in each sentence?

B Look at the words in **bold** and answer the questions about these passive verbs.
- The computer **is programmed** to recognise swimmers.
- Think of your life before the answering machine **was invented**.
- Think of your grandparents' lives before the television and aeroplane **were introduced**.
  1. Which verbs are in the present simple tense?
  2. Which are in the past simple tense?
  3. Who does or did the actions in these sentences? For example, who programmed the computer?
  4. Is it important for the meaning of these sentences to know who does or did the actions?

C Rewrite the sentences above using active verbs.

SEE WORKBOOK UNIT 6

Ideas: The following sentences are from the reading text on the opposite page. Read the sentences and answer the questions.
- Although the human lifeguards had not noticed, 12 large machine eyes deep underwater were watching the whole thing.
- They will watch out for drowning people, for terrorists carrying bombs...

A What do you think the reading text is about?

B What does *they* refer to in the second statement? What else might they watch out for?

C Why are 'they' watching?

3 READING

A Scan the article and answer the questions.

1 How did Jean-François almost drown?
2 How was he saved?
3 What does the writer say that machines will do in future? Give some examples.

B Read the first two paragraphs carefully. Match the words in **bold** with these definitions.

1 when you do not see, feel or think, usually because you are hurt
2 when something electronic makes a short, high sound
3 to go below the surface of the water
4 to sink under water and die

C Read the last paragraph carefully.

1 Explain the meaning of these phrases:
   (a) a baby's breathing
   (b) heart patients
   (c) track children
   (d) monitored by machines
2 What does the writer say is already happening? Do you agree?
3 Which of the systems in the last paragraph do you think are most useful? Explain why.

4 TALK ABOUT IT

Discuss these ideas in pairs.

1 How do you think the writer of the article feels about surveillance technology? How do you feel about it?
2 Act out this roleplay:
   Student A: You are a lifeguard at the Ancenis swimming pool. You are being interviewed by a reporter. Explain how LeRoy was rescued.
   Student B: You are a reporter interviewing the lifeguard. Ask him / her to explain what happened to LeRoy.

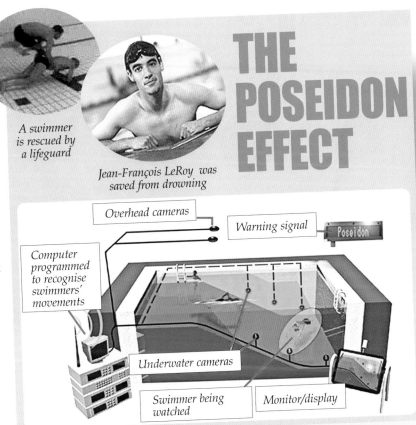

A swimmer is rescued by a lifeguard

Jean-François LeRoy was saved from drowning

THE POSEIDON EFFECT

Overhead cameras
Warning signal
Poseidon
Computer programmed to recognise swimmers' movements
Underwater cameras
Swimmer being watched
Monitor/display

Late one autumn day at the local swimming pool in Ancenis, France, an 18-year-old named Jean-François LeRoy came for his regular evening swim in the 25-metre pool.

When people are **drowning**, they don't usually shout and splash in the way it happens on television. Most people drown quite silently, with the 5 person quickly **sinking** beneath the water. On this evening, LeRoy was testing how far he could swim underwater on one breath. At some moment, as he was doing this, he became **unconscious**. He sank to the bottom of the pool. LeRoy was drowning.

Luckily for him, the swimming pool was installed with an electronic 10 surveillance system called Poseidon. Although the human lifeguards had not noticed, 12 large machine eyes deep underwater were watching the whole thing. Poseidon has underwater cameras which film people as they swim. The cameras are connected to a computer. It is programmed to recognise when a swimmer is not moving normally. The lifeguards at the 15 Ancenis pool were wearing a special device that **beeped** when the computer detected a possible problem. Sixteen seconds after Poseidon noticed LeRoy's body, the lifeguards had pulled him out of the pool. He started breathing again. After one night in the local hospital, he was sent home completely well. Poseidon had saved his life. 20

Machines like Poseidon will completely change how we live. Think of your life before the answering machine was invented. Think of your grandparents' lives before the television and the aeroplane were introduced. The change will be just as great. It is already happening. These days, CCTV cameras are found all over our towns and cities. Each day, 25 thousands of speeding drivers are photographed by speed cameras.

Soon, machines will recognise our faces and our fingerprints. They will watch out for drowning people, for terrorists carrying bombs, for speeding drivers and heart patients. Imagine devices that monitor a baby's breathing and track children as they go to and from school. Imagine machines 30 sending quiet signals to nearby computers, which will send information to your doctor, your lawyer, your car mechanic, the local police. As time passes, more and more of our lives will be monitored by machines. They'll know all about us.

You are being watched

🎧 5 LISTEN IN 🎧

Can RFID tags ...

catch shoplifters ...

... and find lost airline baggage?

A Look at the photos. How do you think that technology can end shoplifting and find lost airline baggage?

B Before you listen to the radio programme, match these words to their definitions.

(a) to trigger (b) item (c) unique
(d) manufacturer (e) to shoplift (f) consumer
(g) constant (h) microchip

1 a very small electronic device, used in computers
2 not the same as anything or anyone else
3 to steal something from a shop
4 a company that makes goods
5 someone who buys things
6 to make a machine start to work
7 happening regularly or all the time

C Listen to the talk about RFID tags. Put the sentences in the correct order by numbering the boxes 1 – 6.

(a) ... each signal is unique ☐
(b) ... the signal from the smart tag will trigger the security system ☐
(c) ... And who's going to use this information? ☐
(d) ... and the tag signal will NOT be killed at checkout ☐
(e) ... 78% of consumers say they don't like the idea of RFID tags ☐
(f) ... could mean that someone somewhere knows where you are ☐

D Were you right in your answer to the question in activity A?

E Listen again. Answer these questions.
1 What are the advantages of RFID tags for businesses?
2 What are the advantages for consumers?
3 What are the disadvantages for consumers?

6 CONTROVERSY

Group A are police and politicians who think that CCTV cameras will help to catch criminals and terrorists. Group B are ordinary people who fear surveillance and loss of privacy.

 SEE ROLE CARDS FOR UNIT 6

7 PORTFOLIO WRITING

Write a short story describing a world where all our movements, phone calls, emails and conversations are monitored. Imagine that the world exists now. Write in the present tense. Indicate whether you like or don't like the idea (170 - 200 words).

Use words and expressions like this:
• Every time we (enter a building), we (are photographed).
• All our phone calls (are recorded).
• All our emails (are read).
• It means that (the government knows everything).
• Terrorism and crime (no longer exist).

8 PHYSICS *in English*

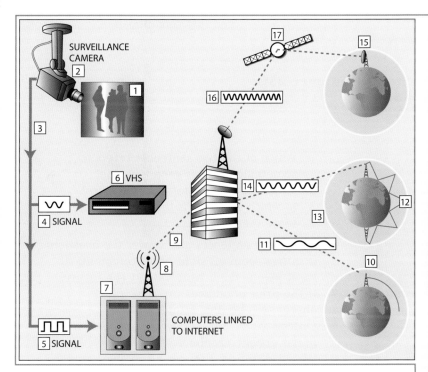

COMMUNICATION WAVES

The images recorded by surveillance cameras can be sent round the world in seconds, using computers. This is what happens. An **image** [1] is produced by a video **camera** [2], and sent along a **cable** [3] as a signal. The signal can be **analogue** [4] or **digital** [5]. Analogue signals are **recorded** [6] on a video cassette (VHS). Digital signals are **stored** [7] on computers linked to the internet. Images are **transmitted** [8] using **radio waves** [9], of which there are three types. **Ground waves** [10] follow the curve of the Earth and have a **long wavelength** [11] (up to 2 MHz). **Sky waves** [12] are reflected by the **ionosphere** [13] and have **medium wavelengths** [14] (3 – 30 MHz). **Space waves** [15] have **short wavelengths** [16] (more than 30 MHz). They are transmitted to **satellites** [17] and back to Earth.

A Read the text. Using the diagram to help you, complete the sentences.
1 Surveillance cameras … the image.
2 … are used to send images round the world.
3 Cables transmit a …
4 There are … types of signal.
5 Computers only store … signals.
6 The three types of radio waves are …
7 … waves have the shortest wavelength.
8 Space waves are … to satellites.

B Make these passive sentences into active sentences.
1 An image is produced by a camera.
2 Digital signals are stored on computers.
3 The image is recorded on a video cassette.
4 Sky waves are reflected by the ionosphere.

9 CONVERSATION

Work in pairs. Use the pictures in this Unit to begin a four-minute discussion about surveillance. Use **Language Bank 12** to help you talk about the pictures. Example:
Student A: • What does this picture show?
Student B: • It's a security camera picture. It shows people standing on a train platform.
Student A: • How do you feel about that?
Student B: • I don't like it but I think it's necessary.
Student A: • Can you say more about that?

10 *Your answer:* IS SECURITY MORE IMPORTANT THAN PRIVACY?

Having read this unit, what do you think? Discuss these questions with the rest of the class. Here are some suggestions to help you with the answers.

A Is security more important than privacy, in your opinion? Explain why / why not.
• Benjamin Franklin said that anyone who gives up liberty to obtain safety deserves neither liberty nor safety.
• Surveillance cameras are only a problem if you are doing something wrong.
• CCTV helped to catch the London terrorists of July 2005.

B What kind of surveillance technology is used in your country?
• CCTV cameras are used on streets and in shops.
• Speed cameras are found on most big roads.

C How do you feel about the use of RFID tags?
• I don't have a problem with it. I think it's very useful.
• You never know how people will use the information. Read George Orwell's book *1984*.

Unit 7   Oil crisis

What's new?

Subject:	Environmental issues
Function:	Speculating, future time expressions
Grammar:	*When, unless, in case,* zero and first conditionals

1   *The BIG question:* WHAT WILL WE DO WHEN THE OIL RUNS OUT?

FACT: Over the last 150 years we have used over 23% of the world's total oil supplies.

2   PREVIEW

Oil well in Siberia, Russia

Wind energy

Solar energy (from the sun)

Words:
Check the meaning of these words and answer the questions.

oil	natural gas	sun	wind	wave
petrol	hydrogen	coal	electricity	

A
1   Which of the above are sources of energy?
2   Which are fuels used in cars or houses?
3   Which are fossil fuels?
4   Which are alternative energy sources?
5   Which are renewable energy sources?

B
1   Which countries are large producers of oil?
2   Which countries are large consumers of oil?

Language:
A   Read these sentences and answer the questions in the next column (above right).

- When oil production starts to go down, prices will go up dramatically.
- When cars burn petrol, they give out carbon dioxide.

1   Which of the two sentences refers to something which is generally true?
2   Which sentence refers to the future?
3   In which sentence is the future simple tense used?

B   Read these sentences and answer the questions.
- If things seem all right at the moment, most people don't worry about the future.
- If the price of oil goes up, renewable energy will become economic.
- Unless we do this, the world will face major energy problems.
- We need to find alternative energy sources, in case the oil runs out.

1   Are the events described in the four sentences above certain to happen?
2   Which of these sentences refers to a general truth? What tenses are used?
3   Which of these sentences refer to the future? What tenses are used?
4   Which word in the third sentence means *if ... not?*
5   Do we use *in case* to refer to:
   (a) something that might happen that we must be ready for?
   (b) something that will definitely happen?

 SEE WORKBOOK UNIT 7

Ideas: The following sentences are from the reading text on the opposite page. Read the sentences and answer the questions.

- "My father rode a camel. I drive a car. My son flies a jet airplane. His son will ride a camel."
- "A drop of petrol in war was worth a drop of blood."
- "The Oil Age will end long before the world runs out of oil."

A   What do you think each of these quotations means?
B   What is your reaction to these statements?
C   In what ways do you use oil?

3 READING

A You are going to read an article about oil. Five sentences have been removed from the text. Choose from the sentences (A)-(F) the one which fits each gap (1)-(5). There is one extra sentence which you do not need to use.

(A) But fewer discoveries of oil are made every year.
(B) We need to find alternative energy sources now, in case the oil runs out sooner than we expect.
(C) It is made from electricity and water.
(D) Most experts agree that we have enough oil for our current needs.
(E) This point is known as Peak Oil.
(F) Bio-fuels do not create pollution in the same way.

Hydrogen power: no pollution

Industry, transport and farming all **run on** oil. And, if things seem all right at the moment, most people don't worry about the future. (1) ... . The world produces 80 million **barrels** of oil a day, and America consumes a quarter of this. It is probable that by 2014, China will consume 14 million barrels a day.

Oil industry experts fear that oil production will 'peak' (reach its greatest amount) between 2010 and 2020. (2) ... . By that time, half of the planet's oil resources will be **used up**. Probably when Peak Oil is past, oil production will go down. If that happens, there could be an oil **crisis** and the price will go up dramatically.

The Oil Age began in America in the 1850s. By World War I, oil was so important that the French Marshal Foch said, 'A **drop** of petrol in war was worth a drop of blood'. Today in Saudi Arabia, which has two thirds of the world's oil, they say: 'My father rode a camel. I drive a car. My son flies a jet airplane. His son will ride a camel."

Many experts believe that if the price of fossil fuels gets too high, renewable energy will become **economic**. (3) ... . Unless we do this, the world will face major energy problems. But not everyone agrees. "**The Stone Age** did not end for lack of stone, and the Oil Age will end long before the world runs out of oil," said Saudi Arabia's past oil minister, Sheikh Yamani.

Wind farms are being built in many countries, such as Denmark and Britain. **Bio-fuels**, like ethanol (alcohol), are made from **crops** such as sugar. In Brazil and Australia, ethanol is added to petrol, so that cars use less oil. When cars burn petrol, they give out **carbon dioxide**, polluting the air. (4) ... .

Many people think that hydrogen is the perfect fuel for the future. (5) ... . If you have enough solar power to make electricity, it can be produced in limitless quantities. When hydrogen burns, it produces no pollution – only a little water vapour. Some car companies are now building hydrogen-powered cars.

C Read the text again and answer the questions about this text.

1 How much of the world's oil does the USA use?
2 When will half the world's oil be used up?
3 Why will "his son ride a camel"?
4 Why is it important to find alternative energy sources now?
5 What renewable energy sources are mentioned here?
6 Why is hydrogen the fuel of the future?

B Scan the text and match the words in **bold** with these definitions.

1 a large container, or a measure of oil
2 time when a situation is very bad
3 plants that farmers grow and sell
4 a gas
5 able to make money
6 a fuel made from plants
7 a small amount of liquid
8 (to) finish or use all of something
9 (to) work by using something
10 a long time ago in human history

4 TALK ABOUT IT

Use **Language Bank 13** to help you give your opinion and speculate about the future.

A What do you think will be the results of oil becoming very expensive?
B When Peak Oil is past, how will things change?
C If Americans use less oil, will the world be more peaceful?
D What can we do personally to use less oil?

🎧 5 LISTEN IN 🔟

A Look at the picture (right).

1 Why do you think this house has:
  (a) solar panels?
  (b) a hydrogen tank?
  (c) a rainwater tank?

2 Is the design of the house traditional or modern?

B You are going to hear a conversation between a journalist called Tony Forbes and Professor Sopian of the Advanced Engineering Centre in Malaysia.
Number the words or phrases that they use, in the order 1–6 as you hear them.

Solar panels on the roof

Rainwater collected from the roof

Hydrogen gas tank in the ground outside

The Solar-hydrogen Eco-house in Malaysia

(a) solar panels	☐	(d) oxygen	☐
(b) air conditioning	☐	(e) stove	☐
(c) pipe	☐	(f) roof	☐

C Listen again. Are these statements true (**T**) or false (**F**)? **T/ F**

1 The professor talks about the house while he is showing Tony around. ☐

2 This is the first house in the world to run on oxygen. ☐

3 Rainwater runs down a pipe to a tank in the garden. ☐

4 The hydrogen is kept in a tank in the garden. ☐

5 It is hot inside the house. ☐

6 The air conditioning is not working. ☐

D Work in pairs or small groups. One of you tells the others:

1 How easy it is to use renewable energy in houses.

2 Why it is a good idea to build more eco-houses.

3 How good or bad it might be to live in an eco-house.

The others ask questions and express the opposite point of view.

6 CONTROVERSY

Pair A are energy company executives who are not worried by the oil crisis. Pair B are environmentalists who are sure that Peak Oil is closer than we think and that we need alternative energy urgently.

 SEE ROLE CARDS FOR UNIT 7

7 PORTFOLIO WRITING

You are a journalist. Write an article for an environmental magazine (170 - 200 words). Use the Journalist's Notes and the information in this unit to help you. See **Language Bank 14** for future time expressions.

Journalist's Notes

Intro:	*World economy runs on oil* *Problem = oil crisis*
Para 1:	*Start using alternative energy*
Para 2:	*Different types of alternative energy*
Para 3:	*Advantages = less pollution* *Problems = alternative technology not good enough yet*
Conclusion:	*Your ideas*

8 CHEMISTRY in English

A Check the meaning of the words and phrases in **bold** in the text below.

B Read both texts quickly and put as many words as you can into these groups:

Gases	Elements	Pollution

How an oil refinery works

- **Crude oil** was formed millions of years ago from microscopic creatures under the sea.
- Oil is mostly formed from **hydrocarbons**.
- These are a chemical combination of two **elements**, carbon and hydrogen.
- When crude oil is heated in a refinery, it divides into different gases and liquids called **fractions**.
- The lightest fractions have the fewest **carbon atoms**. For example, methane (natural gas) has one carbon atom and four hydrogen atoms.
- The heavier fractions are liquids, such as diesel oil, which has 16 carbon atoms.

C Read the texts again and answer the questions.

1 What is crude oil formed from?
2 What are fractions?
3 Which has the fewest carbon atoms, methane gas or diesel oil?
4 What happens when fossil fuels are burnt?
5 What do greenhouse gases do?
6 What happens if you burn PVC?

Oil products	Pollution problems
Crude oil	Pollution from oil rigs, ships at sea.
Natural gas, gasoline *The molecular formula of methane is CH_4*	Burning **fossil fuels** produces gases: • carbon monoxide (CO) • sulphur dioxide (SO_2) • carbon dioxide (CO_2) • nitrogen dioxide (NO_2) These are **greenhouse gases**, which cause **air pollution** and **acid rain** and increase **global warming**.
Plastics, polymers	Burning some plastics, such as PVC, produces a very poisonous gas, dioxin

9 YOUR TOPIC

Work in groups of four, Pair A and Pair B. **See Language Bank 13** for ways of speculating and **Language Bank 14** for future time expressions.

Pair A: Prepare four or five points for a three-minute talk on a topic connected to this unit.

Example:
- Why we must start using renewable energy sources.
- Discuss what you want to say and make notes of the main points.
- Take turns to make the points.

Pair B: Listen carefully to the points made by Pair A. Discuss Pair A's statements and ask questions.

10 Your answer: WHAT WILL WE DO WHEN THE OIL RUNS OUT?

Having read this unit, what do you think? Discuss these questions with the rest of the class. Here are some suggestions to help you:

A How do you feel about the oil crisis?
- It's frightening. Maybe there will be wars about oil.
- Hopefully, there'll be enough oil for a long time.

B What do we need to do if the oil runs out?
- Obviously, we need to find alternative energy sources very soon.

C What are the alternatives to oil?
- There's wind energy and wave energy.

1   *The BIG read:* CAPTAIN CORELLI'S MANDOLIN **by Louis De Bernières**

The novel takes place on the Greek island of Cephallonia, during the Second World War (1939-1945). Invading Italian soldiers are sent to live in the islanders' homes. Corelli, an Italian captain, is living with a Greek doctor and his daughter, Pelagia. There is very little food and the doctor suggests that they hunt for snails for supper. Despite the fact that Corelli is an invader, he and Pelagia begin to fall in love.

2   PREVIEW

Read the introduction above and answer the questions.

A   1   Why is Captain Corelli staying with the doctor?
2   Why is it a problem if the captain and Pelagia fall in love?
3   Why do they all go out hunting for snails?

B   Check the meanings of these words in **bold** in the text opposite.

crawl   tangle   briars   tunnel   paralyse   thorn
murder   strand   vulnerable   kiss   lousy

3   READING

A   Read the text quickly. Choose the best summary:
1   When they all go hunting for snails, Pelagia's clothes get caught in some briars and Captain Corelli cuts her free. They both cry and then kiss for the first time.
2   They go hunting for snails, and Pelagia gets caught in some briars. The captain untangles her. She cries because it has hurt her. They kiss.
3   They go looking for snails. Pelagia's hair gets caught on some briars. The captain succeeds in untangling her from them. She cries and they kiss for the first time.

B   Read Part 1 carefully. Find these phrases and answer the questions.
● ... the impossible tangle of animal runs and briars
● ... there were legions of fat snails
● ... perhaps she had been struck by falling shrapnel
● ... apparently paralysed into a contorted posture
● ... she was clearly in a state of extreme irritation
● A thorn scraped my cheek

1   Were the briars easy to crawl through?
2   Were there a lot of snails?
3   How did Corelli fear that Pelagia had been hurt?
4   Was Pelagia in a comfortable position?
5   Why was Pelagia so irritated?
6   What part of Pelagia was bleeding?

C   Read Part 2 and answer the questions in complete sentences.
1   Why does Pelagia say, "You're squashing my nose"?
2   Why is the captain pleased with himself?
3   What does Pelagia say the captain shouldn't have done?

D   Describe how the captain feels:
1   when he is alone amongst the briars.
2   when he hears Pelagia say, "O, for God's sake."
3   when he finds her with her hair caught.
4   after Pelagia says, "I can't stand it any more."

4   TALK ABOUT IT

A   Do you find the text romantic? Say why / why not.
B   From this extract, how would you describe Captain Corelli's character?
C   Does this extract make you want to read the book? Say why / why not.
D   How do think the story ends? Is it a happy ending?

5   PORTFOLIO WRITING

Write a letter from either Pelagia or Captain Corelli to a friend, describing his / her feelings towards their lover, and the problems that these feelings bring (120 - 150 words).

① So it was that in the evening, an hour before the setting of the sun and shortly before the cooling of the day, Pelagia and her father, Lemoni* and the captain, found themselves **crawling** ⁵ through the impossible **tangle** of animal runs and **briars**. It became apparent in that dingy light that upon the undersides of the lower leaves there were legions of fat snails. The child and the three adults ¹⁰ became so absorbed in their task that they did not notice themselves becoming separated. The doctor and Lemoni vanished down one **tunnel**, and the captain and Pelagia down another. At ¹⁵ some point the captain found himself on his own, and paused for a second to reflect upon the curious fact that he could not remember ever having felt so contented. He breathed deeply and ²⁰ sighed, relaxing back upon his heels. "Ow, o no," came a voice nearby that was undoubtedly Pelagia's. "O, for God's sake."

Horrified by the terrible thought that ²⁵ perhaps she had been struck by falling shrapnel, the captain fell to his hands and knees, and crawled quickly back along his tunnel towards the place from which ³⁰ the exclamation had come.

He found Pelagia, apparently **paralysed** into a contorted posture that had left her neck ricked backwards. She was on her hands and knees, a long thin streak of blood was spreading diagonally ³⁵ across her cheek, and she was clearly in a state of extreme irritation. "Che succede?" he asked, crawling towards her. "Che succede?"

"I've got my hair caught," she replied ⁴⁰ indignantly. "A **thorn** scraped my cheek, and I jerked my head away, and I caught my hair on these briars and I can't untangle it. And don't laugh."

"I'm not laughing," he said, laughing. ⁴⁵ "I was afraid you'd been wounded."

"I am wounded. My cheek stings. If you don't untangle me, I'll **murder** you. Just stop laughing."

"If I don't untangle you, you'll never ⁵⁰

catch me to murder me, will you? Just hold still."

② He was obliged to reach his hands over her shoulders and peer past her ear in order to see what he was doing. She ⁵⁵ found her face pressing into his chest, and she took in the rough texture and dusty aroma of his uniform. "You're squashing my nose," she protested.

Corelli sniffed appreciatively; Pelagia ⁶⁰ always smelled of rosemary. "I might have to cut this," he said, pulling futilely at the black **strands** that had wound themselves about the thorns.

"Ow, ow, stop pulling it about, just be ⁶⁵ careful. And you're not cutting it."

"You're in a very **vulnerable** position," he remarked, "so just try to appear grateful."

He tugged it out, piece by piece, ⁷⁰ ensuring that he let no hairs slide between his fingers to cause her any pain. "I've done it," he said, pleased with himself, and began to draw back. She shook her head with relief, and as the captain's lips ⁷⁵ passed by her cheek, he **kissed** it gently, before the ear.

She touched her fingertips to the site of the kiss, and reproached him. "You shouldn't have done that." ⁸⁰

He knelt back and held her gaze with his own. "I couldn't help it."

"It was taking advantage."

"I'm sorry." They looked at one another for a long moment, and then, for ⁸⁵ reasons that even she could not fathom, Pelagia began to cry.

"What's the matter? What's the matter?" asked Corelli, his face furrowing in consternation. Pelagia's ⁹⁰ tears rolled down her cheeks and fell into the bucket among the snails. "You're drowning them," he said, pointing. "What's the matter?"

She smiled pitifully, set once more to ⁹⁵ crying. Suddenly she blurted out, "I can't stand it any more, not any of it. I'm sorry."

"Everything is **lousy**," agreed the captain, wondering if he too might yield to the temptation to cry. He took her ¹⁰⁰ hands gently in his hands and touched at her tears with his lips. She gazed at him wonderingly, and suddenly they found themselves, underneath the briars, in the sunset, their knees sore and filthy, ¹⁰⁵ infinitely enclosed in their first unpatriotic and secret kiss.

*A little girl who is a friend of the family.

Extract from *Captain Corelli's Mandolin*, by Louis de Bernières, published by Vintage (May 1995). Reprinted by permission of Random House Group Ltd.

What's new?

Subject:	Education
Function:	Persuading and discouraging
Grammar:	Second conditional

1 *The BIG question:* WHY ARE STUDENTS SO STRESSED?

FACT: A 24-hour telephone helpline in Britain receives over 900 calls a year about exam stress. Most are from students aged 12 to 15. Thousands more ask for a leaflet about exam stress.

2 PREVIEW

Words:

A Say what you think is happening in each of the photos. Use the words in the box.

> to take/pass/fail an exam   results
> upset   delighted

Example: • In picture 1, students are
taking ....

B Put the words and phrases into pairs. Explain your reasons for doing so.

1 graduate   (a) degree
2 to revise   (b) test
3 exam   (c) score
4 grade   (d) to do revision
5 diploma   (e) undergraduate

C Work in pairs. Answer these questions.
1 Are you a full-time or part-time student?
2 Where are you studying? School, college, university, or language school?
3 What subject(s) are you studying?
4 Do you intend to continue your studies? If so, where and what will you study?

Language: Read these sentences and then answer the questions.
• If parents were more realistic, young people would be much happier.
• If we do not reform the country's college entrance system, these tragedies will continue.
• If I were you, I wouldn't worry about it.

A Which of these sentences refer to a situation that may happen? What tenses are used?
B Which of these sentences refer to an imaginary situation? What tenses are used? Do these sentences refer to the past?
C What phrase is used to give advice?

SEE WORKBOOK UNIT 8

1

2

3

Ideas: The following sentences are similar to sentences in the reading text opposite. Read the sentences and answer the questions.
• A 19-year-old high school student was so upset about her exam results that she killed herself.
• The girl had just taken the S.A.T. Test.
• The exam more or less decides the level of college that a person can attend.

A Why do you think the high school student killed herself?
B What is your reaction to the first two sentences?
C What is your reaction to the last statement? Are there exams in your country that are extremely important?
D How do you feel about exams? Do you find them stressful?

3 READING

A You are going to read an article about exam stress. Four sentences have been removed from the text. Choose from the sentences (A)-(E) the one which fits each gap (1)-(4). There is one extra sentence which you do not need to use.

(A) It would also mean that parents would spend more money on private education.

(B) It would also mean that parents wouldn't have to spend so much money on private education.

(C) Lee had told her friend that she was worried that she would not be able to go to college because of a low test score.

(D) In Namwon, North Cholla Province, another student died the day before, shortly after taking the first part of the college entrance exam.

(E) They felt that their parents and teachers expected things from them that they could not achieve.

Exam success

Exam failure

Student's exam stress
Seoul, Korea

A 19-year-old high school student killed herself by jumping from the 25th floor of an apartment building in Seoul after becoming distressed about her scores in a test. The student, whose family name was Lee, had just taken the Korea S.A.T., the college entrance exam. Apparently, she had talked ⁵ to a friend about her fears, just before her death. (1) ... .

Unfortunately, Lee is not the first student to kill herself because of exam pressure. (2) ... . It is believed that she also killed herself because she felt she had done very badly in the test. Three other students committed ¹⁰ suicide last month because they feared they would fail.

The college entrance exam more or less decides the level of college that a person can attend, which is why students get so anxious about it. The type of college a student attends then decides the position in society that a person ¹⁵ can reach. 'These young people seem to have had a strong feeling of failure. (3) ... . If parents were more realistic, young people would be much happier,' said Han Sun-ho, professor of psychiatry at Soon Chun Hyang University.

Korean teachers and psychiatrists think that the cause of all ²⁰ these deaths is the college entrance system, and it is a serious and growing problem. The fact that society judges people by their university diploma creates intense competition among students. 'This is very unhealthy,' said Song Won-jae, spokesman for the Korea Teachers and Education Workers ²⁵ Union. 'If we do not reform the country's college entrance system, these tragedies will continue.' He said that if the college entrance exam was easier, students would not need to do so much preparation for the test. (4) ... .

B 1 Read the article carefully. In the second paragraph find words that mean:

(a) sadly   (b) to kill yourself   (c) to be afraid

2 In paragraph 4 find words that mean:

(a) reason   (b) bad for you   (c) change

C Read the second paragraph again. Are these statements true (**T**) or false (**F**)?

T / F

1 Four students have killed themselves in recent months. ☐

2 The latest student to kill herself had just taken the first part of the S.A.T. exam. ☐

3 The student from North Cholla province had done badly in the first part of the test. ☐

D Read the rest of the article. Answer the questions in your own words.

1 Why do students worry about their S.A.T. test score?

2 Why does Professor Han Sun-ho think that these young people committed suicide?

3 What do many teachers feel about the exam?

4 TALK ABOUT IT

A Work in pairs.
Student A: You are preparing for an exam. If you fail, you will not get a university place this year. You are thinking of not taking the exam. Explain your fears to Student B. Start like this:
- If I don't take the exam, I can't fail.
Student B: Listen to your friend, Student A. Persuade and encourage him/her to take the exam. Use **Language Bank 15** to help you do this. Start like this:
- If I were you, I'd ...

B If you had an important exam in four days' time and had done very little revision, how would you feel? What would you do?

C What advice would you give on how to prevent exam stress? Example:
- If you go to bed early the night before the exam, ...

Exam pressure

5 LISTEN IN

A Work in pairs. Check the meaning of the words in **bold** and answer the questions.
1 How much **revision** did you do before your last exams?
2 Have you ever **retaken** an exam?
3 Would you like to be **bilingual**? Explain why/why not.
4 Would you ever see a **counsellor** if you felt stressed?
5 Do you think you would feel **homesick** if you studied abroad?
6 Are there good **job opportunities** in your country for graduates?

B Listen to a conversation between three foreign students who are studying at a top American university. Lufti, Yana and Emiko have just finished their end-of-year exams. Answer these questions.
1 What is Lufti's problem?
2 What is the reaction of Yana and Emiko?

C Listen again. Answer these questions.
1 What do Yana and Emiko say about the advantages of studying in America?
2 Does Yana have friends who are American?
3 How does Emiko feel about her time in America?
4 What suggestion does Emiko make?
5 How do you think each of the students feels at the end of the conversation? Why?

D Work in small groups. Discuss this question: Would you like to study abroad? Say why/why not.

E Work in groups of three. Each person plays one of the roles in the listening passage.
Students A & B: Play the parts of Emiko and Yana. Try to persuade Lufti to stay at university. Use **Language Bank 15** to help you. Student C: Play the part of Lufti. At the end, say if your friends have persuaded you to remain at university.

6 CONTROVERSY

Student A has just passed his or her exams but does not want to go to university. Students B and C are student A's parents. One of you supports A and the other doesn't.

SEE ROLE CARDS FOR UNIT 8

7 PORTFOLIO WRITING

Write a formal letter to a college in America enquiring about ESOL courses (120–150 words).

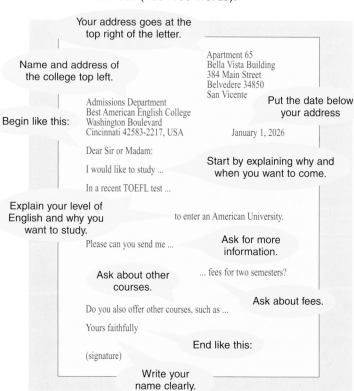

Your address goes at the top right of the letter.

Name and address of the college top left.

Apartment 65
Bella Vista Building
384 Main Street
Belvedere 34850
San Vicente

Put the date below your address

Admissions Department
Best American English College
Washington Boulevard
Cincinnati 42583-2217, USA

Begin like this:

January 1, 2026

Dear Sir or Madam:

I would like to study ...

Start by explaining why and when you want to come.

In a recent TOEFL test ...

Explain your level of English and why you want to study.

to enter an American University.

Please can you send me ...

Ask for more information.

Ask about other courses.

... fees for two semesters?

Do you also offer other courses, such as ...

Ask about fees.

Yours faithfully

(signature)

End like this:

Write your name clearly.

8 EDUCATION *in English*

Harvard, Cambridge, Mass, USA, or Trinity College, Cambridge, UK?

A Check the meaning of these words and phrases. They are all in the text below.

communication	academic	scientific	publish
research	overseas students	journals	talent
enrol	study skills	peers	

B If you took a course in English for Academic Purposes (EAP), what would you study?

Why study EAP?

English has become the language of scientific and academic communication all over the world. English is particularly important for scientific research. As far back as 1981, about 80% of scientific journals were published in English. Today, the figure is much higher. ₅ Scientists publish in English because they want their work to be read by their peers all over the world.

As a result, every year American universities enrol over half a million overseas students to study their subjects in English. It's a business worth almost $13 ₁₀ billion a year to the USA. America depends on foreign talent for research in science and engineering, with over half of all graduate students coming from abroad. Many US universities also provide courses in English for Academic Purposes (EAP), which include subjects ₁₅ such as academic reading and writing, critical thinking, study skills and research.

But now American universities are worried that, after September 11, 2001 and the Iraq war, foreign students do not want to study in the USA. Many prefer ₂₀ to go to Australia or Britain. Also, many European, Middle Eastern and Asian universities now use English as the language of instruction in scientific subjects.

C Read the text. Was your answer to B above correct?

D Read the text again and answer these questions.
1 Why is so much scientific research published in English?
2 Why do so many overseas students study at English-speaking universities?
3 Why do overseas students need courses in EAP?

9 YOUR TOPIC

Work in small groups. Two of you prepare a three-minute talk on a topic that has some connection with this unit. Example:
● Studying abroad.
● Discuss your topics and make a list of your main points.
● Begin by introducing the talk.
● During your talk, try to give some examples of what you mean.
● Ask your listeners two or three questions about the topic.
● The other two listen carefully. They ask questions and ask for examples where relevant.

See **Language Bank 16** for ways of asking for and giving examples.

10 *Your answer:* WHY ARE STUDENTS SO STRESSED?

Having read this unit, what do you think? Discuss these questions with the rest of the class. Here are some suggestions to help you with the answers.

A Why do students get so stressed?
● They get stressed because of pressure from their parents.
● Because they know how important exams are.

B Would you feel homesick if you went abroad to study? If so, what would you do about it?
● Yes, I'm sure I'd really miss my friends.
● I'd write long emails to my family.

C What would you do if you felt very stressed before an important exam?
● I'd see a counsellor.
● I'd take a lot of exercise.

Unit 9 — Give peace a chance

What's new?

Subject:	Personal values and ideals
Function:	Adding and contrasting information
Grammar:	Cohesive devices

1 *The BIG question:* CAN WE STOP WARS?

FACT: There is one gun for every 12 people in the world. 90% of people killed by small arms are civilians. 800 people are killed by land mines every month.

2 PREVIEW

Words:

A Work in groups. Which of these things are used by the army, the air force or the navy? Some of them are used by more than one armed service.

aircraft carriers   rifles   tanks
helicopters   machine guns   missiles

B Look at the photographs on these two pages and answer the questions.

1 Who uses small arms (guns like the AK-47 rifle)?
2 Which countries suffer from land mines?
3 Why do you think there are so many civilian victims in wars?
4 What do you know about other weapons not listed above?

Language: Read the sentences, then answer the questions about the words and phrases in **bold**.

- **Furthermore**, there are now ten times as many AK-47s in the world as M16s.
- **However**, Kalashnikov takes no responsibility for the victims of his invention.
- **Consequently**, it was like a genie out of the bottle.
- **On the other hand**, sometimes it is out of control.
- **Meanwhile**, the weapon is still produced in the same factory.

A Which of the words in **bold** indicate an additional idea or argument?
B Which of them indicate that a contrasting idea is following? (2 answers)
C Which of them indicate a result?
D Which one indicates that something else is happening at the same time?

SEE WORKBOOK UNIT 9

AK-47 rifle

Clearing land mines in Afghanistan

US Navy aircraft carrier

Ideas: The following sentences are from the reading text on the opposite page. Read them and answer the questions.

- Mikhail Kalashnikov is very proud of his invention (the AK-47 assault rifle).
- Designing a weapon is like a woman having a child.
- The fact that people die because of an AK-47 is not because of the designer, but because of politics.

A Do you think the inventor of a gun should be proud of it?
B What do you think of the comparison between designing a weapon and having a child?
C Do you think the designer of a weapon can blame politicians for the effects of the weapon?

42

3   READING

A   Before you read the text, tell other students anything you know about Mikhail Kalashnikov and/or his invention, the AK-47 rifle.

> **Mikhail Kalashnikov was born in 1919, the seventeenth child of a Russian peasant family. He invented the Kalashnikov automatic rifle, the most successful small weapon in the history of warfare.**

'I SLEEP SOUNDLY'

In 1947, the Avtomatni Kalashnikova (Kalashnikov Automatic) won a Soviet competition for a submachine gun for the Red Army. Fifty-six years, more than 100 million guns and many millions of dead later, it remains **the world's most successful killing machine.** Even so, the 5 inventor Mikhail Kalashnikov is very proud of his creation.

"You see, designing a weapon is like a woman having a child," he says. "For months she carries her baby and thinks about it. A designer does much the same thing with a weapon. I felt like a mother - always proud. It is a special 10 feeling, as if you were given a special award."

Kalashnikov guns probably caused most of the **300,000 annual combat deaths** in the **wars and conflicts of the 1990s.** They were the **primary weapon** in almost all the 40-plus wars of that decade. 15 Furthermore, there are now ten times as many AK-47s in the world as M16s, their American rival. The Soviet government also gave many of them away to friendly governments and revolutionary fighters.

However, Kalashnikov takes no responsibility for 20 the victims of his invention. "I made it to protect the motherland. And then they spread the weapon around the world. It was not my choice. Consequently, it was like **a genie out of the bottle** and it began to walk all on its own and in directions I did not want." 25

Even so, "the positive outweighs the negative," he insists, "because many countries use it to defend themselves. On the other hand, sometimes it is out of control. **Terrorists also want simple and reliable arms.** Nevertheless, I sleep soundly. The fact that people die 30 because of an AK-47 is not because of the designer, but because of politics."

Meanwhile, the weapon is still produced in the same factory in Izhevsk, which is now a tourist attraction. In a local hotel, an American tourist wears an 35 "AK-47 World Destruction Tour" T-shirt. The list of places visited on the tour include Chechnya, Afghanistan, the Gaza Strip, the Congo, etc. In one of the town's gun shops, Liliya, aged 12, and her friend stand and stare at the AK-47s on display. "It's our first 40 time here," she says. "We just wanted to see."

BY NICK PATON WALSH, THE GUARDIAN

B   Scan the text and say what the following dates and numbers refer to:

| 1919 | 1947 | 100 million | 300,000 | 40-plus |

C   Read the text more carefully and explain the phrases in **bold**, using your own words.

D   Answer these questions about words and expressions from the text.

I sleep soundly.	1	Does this mean he sleeps well or makes a lot of noise when he sleeps?
The Soviet government gave many of them away	2	Does this mean that the guns were free or that they were thrown away?
The positive outweighs the negative	3	Does this mean there are more good things about it, or more bad things?

4   TALK ABOUT IT

Work in pairs or small groups. **Use Language Bank 17.** Start with one of the questions below and take turns to add and/or contrast more facts and ideas.

A   Would you like to visit the AK-47 factory in Izhevsk?

B   Is it only terrorists who use Kalashnikov weapons?

C   Should the factory in Izhevsk continue to produce the AK-47?

D   Do you think we could stop war by stopping the manufacture of small arms?

Give peace a chance

5 LISTEN IN 9

A You are going to hear part of a radio programme called *Peace News*. Before you listen, answer these questions.

1 What do you know about the Gaza Strip?
2 If someone is a peace activist, what do you think they do?

B 1 Use your dictionary to find the correct definitions of these words.

A peace activist stands in front of an Israeli bulldozer in the Gaza Strip

Two million people demonstrating in Rome against war in Iraq

volunteer   civilian target
to have an effect   immoral
occupation (of territory)   conflict
injury   tragic incident

2 After reading this list of words and expressions, what kind of information do you expect to hear about? How do you think the words and expressions will be used?

C Listen to the radio programme. Were your predictions about the programme right?

D Give your reactions to the stories in the programme.

1 Why was Rachel Corrie run over by a bulldozer?
2 How would you describe what Tom Hurndall was doing when he was shot?
3 What do you think of the actions of the Israeli pilots?
4 Was the demonstration in London special in any way?

6 CONTROVERSY

Work in groups of four. Debate the following statement:
- You have a right not to fight in a war if it is immoral.

Two students defend this statement and two oppose it. Support your partner's arguments.

 SEE ROLE CARDS FOR UNIT 9

7 PORTFOLIO WRITING

Write an article for a peace magazine. Describe in your own words any of the events mentioned in this unit (170 - 200 words).

Try to include the following:	Example:
1 A short, clear, interesting headline	• A moral war?
2 An interesting introduction	• He was the seventeenth child.
3 Two or three paragraphs with your opinions and the reasons for them.	• In my opinion, a country has the right to defend itself in any way, because ...
4 Examples to support your opinion	• For instance, if land mines help to defend ...
5 Arguments for the other side	• On the other hand, peace is always better than war.
6 A conclusion	• In conclusion, I would say that ...

8 PEACE STUDIES *in English*

A Before you read the text:
1 Share with other students anything you know about the following.
- The United Nations (UN)
- The Nobel Peace Prize
- The Cold War
- The Bosnian War in the 1990s

2 Try to predict which countries provide the most UN peacekeepers.
3 Then scan the text to find out which countries really do.

KEEPING THE PEACE

If you see soldiers wearing sky-blue helmets in a conflict zone, they are peacekeepers from the United Nations. UN peacekeeping operations were the idea of Canadian Foreign Minister Lester Pearson, who won the Nobel Peace Prize for his work.

The first UN peacekeeping mission was in 1948, after the first Arab–Israeli conflict. Since then, there have been more than 50 operations. Since the end of the Cold War, the number of UN peacekeeping operations has increased dramatically. In 2003, there were fifteen, involving 37,000 personnel.

Nearly 130 countries have contributed personnel to UN peacekeeping operations. Since 2000, the main contributors have been Pakistan, Bangladesh, India and Ghana. Other important contributors are the Scandinavian countries, plus Finland, Canada, Fiji, Ireland, Italy and Australia. Recently Eastern European countries such as Poland and the Czech Republic also became involved.

The mid-1990s saw two of the UN's greatest failures. The genocide in Rwanda in 1995 occurred despite warnings of the dangers. About half a million people died. Similarly, in Bosnia, UN peacekeepers were unable to protect civilians. More than 7,000 Muslims were killed at Srebrenica.

B Read the text and find the following:
1 Where was the first UN peacekeeping mission?
2 Whose idea were UN peacekeeping operations?
3 Name two places where the UN failed.

C Which of these opinions do you agree or disagree with? Say why.
1 UN peacekeepers should go to more places where there is conflict.
2 The UN cannot stop all wars.

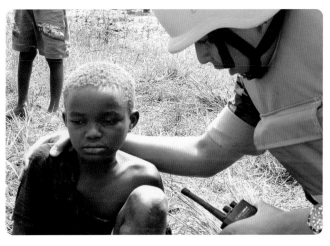

A UN soldier comforts a child in Congo, Africa

9 INTERACTIVE TASK

Work in groups of four, Pair A and Pair B. Make a list of points to discuss on this topic:
- Do you have a right to kill in self-defence?
- If so, under what circumstances?

Pair A: Take turns to discuss the question.
Pair B: Take turns to make comments and try to take control of the discussion, for example:

Student A: • If someone attacks you, I think you have a right to defend yourself.

Student B: • Of course you do, but do you have a right to kill your attacker?

Student C: • I think you have a right to kill if your attacker has a gun.

Student D: • However, if he doesn't, that's a different matter.

See **Language Bank 17** for cohesive words.

10 *Your answer:* CAN WE STOP WARS?

Having read this unit, what do you think? Discuss these questions with the rest of the class. Here are some suggestions to help you:

A Are some wars necessary?
- Yes. It is important to stop genocide or terrorism.
- No. It's possible to solve all problems by negotiations.

B What can ordinary people do to stop wars?
- We can vote for politicians who support peace.
- Nothing. Ordinary people have no power.

C Should the UN do more?
- Yes. More people trust the UN.
- No. UN soldiers' lives are in danger.

What's new?

Subject: Society and living standards
Function: Expressing wishes and hopes
Grammar: Verb patterns after *wish* and *hope*

1 *The BIG question:* HOW MUCH IS ENOUGH?

FACT: There are over 9.5 million US dollar millionaires in the world. Meanwhile, over 2.8 billion people live on less than two dollars a day.

2 PREVIEW

Words:

A Which of these are luxuries and which are necessities?

| computer | video camera | holidays |
| clothes | television | shoes |

B Look at photos 1 and 2:
1 What kind of food is in the photo and who eats it?
2 What is a luxury food for you?
3 Where do people have problems getting drinking water?

C Look at photos 3 and 4:
1 Is a car a luxury or a necessity?
2 Is the car in the photo a luxury car?
3 Is a yacht a luxury?
4 Would you like to own a yacht like this?

D 1 Number these items in order of importance in your life. In groups, compare your answers.

| mp3 player (iPod) | hi-fi | microwave oven |
| washing machine | dishwasher | mobile phone |

2 What can you buy with a million dollars?
3 What can you buy with $2 a day?

Language: Read these sentences and answer the questions.
- He is hoping to start a business.
- I hope one of them offers me a place.
- I wish they wouldn't fight all the time.
- I wish I had a TV in my room.
- I wish we hadn't moved.

Which sentence refers to:
A something that you think may happen?
B situations that are impossible or unlikely?
C the present?
D the past?
E the future?
F an activity in the present that someone is choosing to do?

food

2

car

water *yacht*

Ideas: The following sentences are from the reading text on the opposite page. Read them and answer the questions.
- They took luxury holidays and their million-pound house contained all the gadgets that money could buy.
- All my friends got iPods for Christmas, but mum said we couldn't afford one! I mean, they're only a couple of hundred pounds!

A Does the family in the first sentence sound like a happy family? Say why/why not.
B What is your reaction to the second sentence?

 SEE WORKBOOK UNIT 10

3 READING 🔘

A Scan the text and answer these questions.
1 Does downshifting mean making things smaller?
2 How does the family feel about downshifting?

1 Rupert and Emma Wood used to live in London. Rupert worked as a banker and Emma was a successful lawyer. 5 Between them they earned over £150,000 a year. Their four children were all at 10 expensive private schools. They took luxury holidays and their million-pound house contained all the 15 gadgets that money could buy.

But Rupert and Emma were always stressed and spent very little time with each other or the children. A year ago, they decided to downshift. They 20 gave up their jobs and moved to Llanrhystud, a village on the west coast of Wales. Rupert is hoping to start a business as a financial advisor. Emma looks after the house and works part-time in her daughter's school, where the children are taught the Welsh language. 25

2 I went to Llanrhystud to interview them. Their house has the same number of rooms as their former house in London, but cost them a quarter of the price. When I arrived, the family had just returned from a walk on the beach. Emma prepared lunch and Rupert took me to see 30 the garden, which is enormous, and has a panoramic view of the nearby hills. While we were in the garden, one of their children, 12-year-old Paul, came out to feed the ducks. "I don't really like this job," he said. "I wish they wouldn't fight all the time." 35

The Wood family moved from London to a country cottage in Wales

3 I asked them to tell me how their lives had changed. Eight-year-old Daphne seemed very happy. "I've got lots of new friends at school and I'm hoping to get a dog." Apart from his problem with the ducks, Paul is also 40 happy in Llanrhystud. "I can ride my bike to the beach – and that's SO cool!" he said.

However Melissa, who is 15, and Joel, 17, are having problems adjusting to their new life. Melissa likes the house but isn't happy about other things. "All my friends 45 in London got iPods for Christmas, but mum said we couldn't afford one!" she said, "I mean, they're only a couple of hundred pounds!" Anything else? " Yes, I wish I had a TV in my room."

Joel is not happy at all. " I wish we hadn't moved. 50 There's nothing to do," he said. "I miss London, and the kids round here …." He didn't finish the sentence, but I got the meaning. "This is my last year in school, thank God! I've applied to three universities in London. I hope one of them offers me a place. If I have to stay and 55 speak Welsh, I'll go crazy."

B Read part 1 and answer these questions.
1 Why did Rupert and Emma decide to downshift?
2 What were their lives like before they moved?
3 What has changed since they moved?

C Read part 2 and complete the sentences.
1 Their new house is ......
2 In the garden, you can see ......
3 Paul is unhappy because ......

D Read part 3 and say who:
1 is hoping to get a dog.
2 wishes she had a TV in her room.
3 hopes to leave as soon as possible.

4 TALK ABOUT IT

Use **Language Bank 18** to help you answer the questions. Work in groups.
1 Has anyone in the class moved from another place in the last few years? Is there anything you miss? State your feelings like this:
• I wish there was more to do in this town.
2 What consumer gadgets, like an iPod, do you wish you had? What things do you hope to have in the next year, 5 years, 10 years?
3 Rupert and Emma decided that time is more valuable than money. What is your opinion?

5 LISTEN IN

A You are going to listen to two radio reports on the garbage economy. What connection does this have to the photograph?

B Before you listen, match the words to their definitions.
(a) scavenging
(b) rubbish (*BrE*) dump
(c) garbage (*AmE*)
(d) one-room shack
(e) foul smell
(f) used syringes
(g) toxic fumes
(h) rotting meat

1 place where people take unwanted things
2 badly built small house
3 very bad smell
4 searching through rubbish for useful things
5 food that has gone bad
6 things that have been thrown away
7 plastic tube and needle used for injections
8 poisonous gas

C With a partner discuss how you think these words and expressions fit into reports about the garbage economy.

D Listen to the complete programme and answer the questions.
1 Which countries are the reporters in?
2 How far are the dumps from the nearest big cities?
3 Are both cities the capitals of their countries?
4 How many people work at the first dump?
5 What kinds of things do the scavengers collect?
6 Are the scavengers organised in any way?
7 How much money do the scavengers make?
8 What are the scavengers hoping for?
9 Why is scavenging dangerous?

E In small groups, discuss the similarities and differences between the styles of the two reports.

6 CONTROVERSY

Get into groups of four and debate the subject:
● Poverty is the most important problem in the world.

 SEE ROLE CARDS FOR UNIT 10

7 PORTFOLIO WRITING

You have received an email from someone of your age who is coming to live near you. He or she comes from a country where things are very cheap and is worried about how much basic things will cost. Write an email (120 - 150 words) saying how much the following things cost:
● rent or the cost of somewhere to live
● entertainment – clubs, cinemas, bars
● local transport – bus, metro, tram
● clothes – jeans, t-shirts, shirts/blouses
● cup of coffee in a café
● food and other necessities

8 SOCIAL STUDIES in English

Child poverty in Britain

In the UK 3.5 million children are living in poverty. In 1983, 14% of all UK households lacked three or more essential items, because people couldn't afford them. This number increased to over 24% by 1999. In other words, a quarter of the British population was living in poverty at the end of the twentieth century. Essential items mean 'items that more than 50% of people believe they should be able to afford'. These include washing machines and televisions. Mobile phones are not seen as essential items. Since 1999 a government campaign has lifted 600,000 British children out of poverty. But one in three poor children still go without proper shoes and a winter coat. They miss out on toys and after-school activities, and they live five to six years less than rich children.

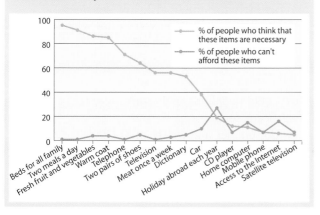

A Scan the text and answer these questions.
1 What is the definition of items that are a necessity? Give examples.
2 Do the following expressions mean more or less the same thing?

- can't afford
- do without
- miss out on
- lack

B Read the list of items on the graph (below left) and put them in your own order, starting with most essential (number 1) and ending with the least essential (number 16).

9 CONVERSATION

In pairs, hold a four-minute discussion on one of these topics:
A Student A chooses a photo from this unit:
- What does this picture show?
- How do you feel about it?
 Student B looks at the photo and reacts to it:
- It shows that some people don't even have water.
- I feel shocked by the photo of the scavengers.
 Use **Language Bank 12** to help ask about and describe pictures.

B People in Britain think that a washing machine is a necessity. What do you think people who live on less than $2 a day think about that? Explain their point of view.

C People are often poor because they have other problems. They don't speak the main language well, for example. What do you think causes poverty?
 Use **Language Bank 19** to check that you understand each other correctly.

10 Your answer: HOW MUCH IS ENOUGH?

Having read this unit, what do you think? Discuss these questions with the rest of the class. Here are some suggestions to help you.
A How much is enough for you personally?
- I hope to own my home.
- I wish I had enough money to have two holidays a year.
B Does money make you happy?
- Yes, of course!
- If you don't have money, life is very difficult.
C When we say someone is rich, what do we mean?
- I think we mean someone who has a lot of luxuries.
- Someone who doesn't need to work.

What's new?

Subject: Habits and obsessions
Function: Evaluating options
Grammar: *though, even though, although, in spite of, despite*

1 *The BIG question*: ARE PEOPLE GETTING BIGGER?

FACT: More than a quarter of the people in the world (1.2 billion) are overweight. Of these, 300 million are obese.

obese

overweight

slim

2 PREVIEW

Words:
A Which of the words and pictures above fits these definitions?
1 Heavier than you should be for good health.
2 Heavier than you want to be for comfort.

B Look at the photos and discuss these questions.
1 Do these photographs show ordinary people?
2 What differences can you imagine between the lifestyles of these people?

C Do you agree (A) or disagree (D)?   A/D
1 It's easy to avoid getting overweight.   ☐
2 It's very easy to be obsessed with food.   ☐
3 It's a bad idea for young people to go on   ☐
   a diet.
4 Slimmer people are healthier than heavier   ☐
   people.
5 You can get fat even if you don't eat too   ☐
   much.

Language: Read these sentences and answer the questions.

• **Although** Houston residents agree the statistics are true, they don't like being described in this way.
• Dallas also has plenty of junk food **though**, including 105 doughnut shops.
• **Even though** Houston folk can't do anything about the poor air quality, they could turn off the TV and get out to the parks.
• In Houston, people don't do enough exercise and sport, **in spite of** the fact that the city's sports facilities are excellent.

A Do the words in **bold** mean more or less the same thing?
B Which of the words or phrases in **bold** is the most formal?
C Which word or phrase is most emphatic?
D Rewrite the second sentence using the word *but*.
E Rewrite the last two sentences as two separate sentences each, using *however*.

SEE WORKBOOK UNIT 11

Ideas: The following sentences are from the reading text on the opposite page. Read them and answer the questions below.

• Unless we start worrying about how fat we are, we will have a really serious problem, particularly for our healthcare services.
• Fit US cities ... don't have to deal with sultry summers and arctic winters.
• Houston is fat, but so is every other city. We are a fat society.

A How could people's weight have an effect on healthcare services?
B How do summer and winter affect people who want to keep fit?
C Do you think the last sentence describes your society?

3   READING

A   Use the title and the photographs to predict the contents of the article.

B   Before you read the whole article, decide on the more likely meaning of these sentences.
- *We don't plan to pick on any particular city.*
   1   (a) We don't intend to criticise one particular place.
       (b) We don't plan to visit a particular city.
- *Fit US cities tend to be out west.*
   2   (a) Fit people often live in cities in the west of the USA.
       (b) Fit people often move to cities in the west of the USA.
- *Colorado's climate and mountains attract people who care about their health.*
   3   (a) When people move to Colorado, they begin to care about their health.
       (b) People who care about their health move to Colorado because of the environment.

In Colorado Springs …

In Houston …

… people are the fittest in America

…people are the fattest in America

Houston, We Have a Big Problem

by Nanci Hellmich

Oh no, not again! Houston has been named the fattest city in the USA for the second year in a row by **Men's Fitness** magazine.

Although Houston residents agree the statistics are true, they don't like being described in this way. "All cities are fat. To choose one is silly," says John Foreyt, an obesity expert at Baylor College of Medicine in Houston. "Yes, Houston is fat, but so is every other city. We are a fat society." In fact, 61% of Americans are overweight, and about 27% of them are obese – 30 pounds or more (about 13.5 kilos) above a healthy weight. [10]

"We don't plan to pick on any particular city," says editor-in-chief, Jerry Kindela. "But the fact is, unless we start worrying about how fat we are, we will have a really serious problem, particularly for our healthcare services." [15]

Fit US cities tend to be out west and don't have to deal with sultry summers and arctic winters, and the residents also think fitness is important, the magazine says.

James Hill, an obesity researcher at the University of Colorado, says Colorado's climate and natural [20] resources, including the mountains, attract people [25] who care about their health and fitness habits. "It's a culture that values these things," he says.

The magazine gives possible reasons for the statistics. In Houston, people watch too much TV and don't do enough exercise and sport, in spite of the fact that the [30] city's facilities are excellent. "Even though Houston folk can't do anything about the poor air quality, they could turn off the TV and get out to the parks," the editors write.

Chicago has the worst climate of the 50 cities in the survey. Summers are hot and humid; winter has nearly [35] 90 days of below-freezing temperatures. Dallas has four times more restaurants per person than New York, and some of them are among the best in the country. It also has plenty of junk food, though, including 105 doughnut shops. [40]

The city whose residents take the most exercise is Colorado Springs, and people there don't watch much TV either.

C   Read the article carefully and answer these questions. Use your own words in your answers.
   1   What is the reaction of Houston residents to the statistics?
   2   According to the article, why do cities get to the top of the fat chart?
   3   What are the differences in the habits of people in fit cities and fat cities?

4   TALK ABOUT IT

Look at **Language Bank 20** for ways of evaluating options.

A   What could fat city residents do to get fit? Suggest at least five options.
   Examples: • They could go to the parks.
              • They could go jogging.

B   Which options are the best, in your opinion? Explain why.

5   LISTEN IN

A Look at the list of food items. Which of them are fattening?

apples	ham	pizza	biscuits	chocolate bars
cream	spaghetti	cheese	breakfast cereal	ice cream
salad	orange juice			

B Check the meaning of the words in **bold** below. Then work in pairs and discuss the questions.
1 Have you ever **gone on a diet**? If so, did you lose weight?
2 Do you **put on weight** easily, or can you eat what you like?
3 Do you eat **regular meals** or do you **miss** meals and **eat snacks**?
4 Do you want to be **slimmer**, or as you are now?
5 Do you ever feel **faint with hunger**? What do you do about it?

C Listen to Elaine's audio diary. Answer the questions.
1 Why does Elaine decide to diet?
2 What do we learn about her colleague Craig?
3 Is Elaine's diet successful?
4 At the end of Elaine's diary, what does she decide about the diet?
5 Is Elaine obsessed with diets?

D Listen again. Tick ✓ the correct boxes.

Elaine's diary	Mon	Tues	Wed	Thurs	Fri	Sat
1 Elaine eats too much on …						
2 Elaine eats chocolate on …						
3 Elaine finds she has put on a kilo on …						
4 Elaine decides she must lose four kilos on …						

E Work in small groups. Discuss these questions.
1 Do you think Elaine eats well or healthily? Say why / why not.
2 Why do you think she has problems with her weight?
3 What advice would you give her about her relationship with Craig?

Elaine buys a drink for Craig

6   CONTROVERSY

Work in groups of three. Student A is on a diet, takes a lot of exercise and is worried about being fat. Students B and C are his or her parents, who are worried that A is dieting and exercising too much and may become anorexic.

 SEE ROLE CARDS FOR UNIT 11

7   PORTFOLIO WRITING

Work in small groups. Write an advertising brochure for a new Fitness Club in Houston, Texas. Include details of facilities, opening times and prices (170–200 words).

Examples:
Name of your club: *Fat-or-Fit*
Photos: Before and After photos of someone who works out
Facilities of the club: Gymnasium, swimming pool, weights, sauna
Advertisement: *Fat-or-fit* – Your choice for life!
Selling points: Join now – get a 50% reduction in price
Contact details: Tel: 0738 298177
Website: www.fat-or-fitness.com

8 HEALTH EDUCATION *in English*

The future is fat

Childhood obesity, like adult obesity, is caused by an imbalance between
5 calories-in and calories-out – in other words, what you eat and how you use energy to
10 burn it off. All over the world, there is evidence that we are losing the battle to get this
15 simple equation right. The problem is particularly affecting children.

Western Europe: About half of all adults may be obese by 2030.

England: Only 45% of boys and 37% of girls aged 11 take exercise for 2 hours a week or more. 22% of men and 23% of women are obese.

China: 10% of children of wealthy people who live in cities are obese.

NORTH AMERICA

EUROPE

ASIA

AFRICA

Malaysia: 1998 survey said 17% of boys and 8% of girls are obese.

USA: 60 million people are obese.

SOUTH AMERICA

AUSTRALASIA

Chile: 30% of children are overweight or obese.

ANTARCTICA

Australia: Approx 20% of children and teenagers are overweight or obese.

Developing countries in Africa: The poor suffer hunger and malnutrition, while the rich suffer from obesity.

A Check the meaning of these words. Discuss what you know about them already.
1 **globesity:** a new word combining *globe* and *obesity*.
2 **calorie:** a unit for measuring how much energy you get from food.
3 **malnutrition:** an illness caused by not eating enough food, or not eating food with enough calories.

B Read the text and answer these questions.
1 Is obesity restricted to particular parts of the world?
2 Explain what is meant by an *imbalance between calories-in and calories-out*.
3 How is it possible that there is malnutrition and obesity in the same country?

9 YOUR TOPIC

A Conduct a survey of the diet and exercise habits of your class or your friends and family.
1 Do you eat breakfast in the morning?
2 How much fruit do you eat a day?
3 What kind of exercise do you do?
4 Have you made any changes in your eating or exercise habits recently?

B Work in pairs. Student A prepares and gives a four-minute talk about the survey and its results. Make notes about what you want to say.
Introduce your subject like this:
• We conducted a survey …
Be prepared to ask and answer questions.
Student B asks relevant questions. If Student A says something you don't understand, ask for clarification, using **Language Bank 5**.

10 *Your answer:* ARE PEOPLE GETTING BIGGER?

Having read this unit, what do you think? Discuss these questions with the rest of the class. Here are some suggestions to help you.
A Are there are a lot of big people in your country?
• Yes. I think a lot of people in my country eat a lot.
• No. People in my country are fairly healthy.
B Is there a lot of fast food available in your country?
• Yes, there are more and more fast food restaurants.
• No, we don't have many fast food restaurants.
• No, we like food cooked in the traditional way.
C Do people in your country take enough exercise?
• Yes, we take a lot of exercise.
• No, we don't take enough exercise.

What's new?

Subject:	Design
Function:	Eliciting further information
Grammar:	Present perfect passive, future simple passive

1 **The BIG question:** WHERE WILL WE ALL LIVE?

FACT: Already half of the world's population lives in cities. By 2030, five billion people will live in cities.

2 PREVIEW

Swiss architects Herzog & de Meuron designed the Allianz Arena in Munich

Words:

A 1 Look at the photos. What type of buildings do they show?

(a) high-rise accommodation
(b) office building
(c) shopping centre   (d) sports stadium
(e) leisure/entertainment centre
(f) museum/art gallery

B 1 Why is the building in Prague called *Ginger and Fred*?
  2 Think of names for the other two buildings.

C 1 What are the most important criteria for architects to think about when designing buildings? Choose from this list.

(a) accessibility (transport links)
(b) green areas (parks, trees)   (c) beauty
(d) use of space   (e) location   (f) safety

The Ginger and Fred *building in Prague was designed by American Frank Gehry*

  2 Talk about the buildings in the pictures using the criteria above.
  3 Are they good or bad designs for buildings? Why?

The Sydney Opera House was designed by Danish architect Joern Utzon

Language: Read these sentences and answer the questions.

• Two astonishing projects that **have been shown** (on TV) are buildings **that may be built** in Japan.
• If it goes ahead, it **will be built** in the sea, in Tokyo Bay.
• The skyscrapers **will be linked** by a series of hollow tubes.

A What do the verb forms in **bold** have in common?
B Why are these sentences NOT written with active verbs? For example:
• Buildings that someone may build in Japan.
C Which of the sentences reads well with an active verb?

 SEE WOOKBOOK UNIT 12

Ideas: The following sentences are from the reading text on the opposite page. Read them and answer the questions below.

• One of the most amazing projects is Sky City, a 1.6 kilometre-high building.
• It is possible that some residents would never leave it.
• The pyramid will be built by spider robots, and power will be provided by waves and wind.

A What is unusual about these projects?
B How would you feel about never leaving the building where you live?
C Would you be happy living in a pyramid built by spider robots?
D For you, what would be the best and worst things about these buildings?

3 READING   ⑬

A Scan the two articles and find out which of Sky City [S], or Pyramid City [P]:
1 would house more people? ☐
2 would be taller? ☐
3 would be built in the sea? ☐

There is a programme on the Discovery TV Channel called *Extreme Engineering*, which takes an imaginative look at new developments in design. Two astonishing projects that have been shown on the programme are buildings that may be constructed in Japan.

① **1.6 KM-HIGH SKY CITY**

With less and less available building space, Japan is considering some dramatic ways to provide new accommodation for its population. One of the most amazing projects is Sky City, a 1.6 kilometre-high building. If it goes ahead, it will be built in the 5 sea, in Tokyo Bay. It will be the biggest building on earth, more than twice as high as any existing building.

Sky City would have 560 floors, consisting of 14 steel, concrete and glass sections, each 40 10 floors high, one on top of the other. The vertical city would house more than 35,000 people, and provide offices, shops, schools and even parks for another 100,000. Accommodation, work and leisure facilities would all be in the same 15 building, so it is possible that some residents would never leave it. There is only one problem. No one knows for sure if it can be built!

25

B Read Part 1 carefully and write questions for these answers, for example:
● **Q:** How high will Sky City be?
● **A:** Sky City will be 1.6 kilometres high.
1 Q: ....
   A: In the sea, in Tokyo Bay.
2 Q: ....
   A: Twice as high as any existing building.
3 Q: ....
   A: 35,000 people.
4 Q: ....
   A: No, there will also be shops and offices.

②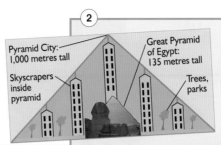

LIVING IN A PYRAMID

Pyramid City is an even more ambitious project to solve Tokyo's housing problem. It would also be situated in Tokyo Bay. A 1,000-metre tall pyramid, twelve times 5 higher than the Great Pyramid of Giza in Egypt, it would contain 55 smaller pyramids, each one the size of the Giza original.

If it is built, the pyramid will consist of a series of skyscrapers suspended from the inside of the structure. The pyramid 10 will be 80 storeys high, with parkland in-between the skyscrapers. Three quarters of a million people will live there. The skyscrapers will be linked by a series of hollow tubes containing a high-speed transport system. Parts of the construction, including more than 150 kilometres of tunnels, 15 will be built by spider robots, and power will be provided by waves and wind.

A major problem is that Japan is situated on the seismic 'ring of fire' – an area of volcanic activity which stretches around the Pacific Ocean. Pyramid City will have to withstand 20 earthquakes, tsunamis and underwater volcanic eruptions. The designers of Pyramid City are certain that it will be built and made safe from earthquakes, but probably not for another 100 years!

C Read Part 2 carefully and decide if these statements are true (**T**) or false (**F**). **T / F**
1 Pyramid City will be the same height as the Great Pyramid of Egypt. ☐
2 There will be smaller pyramids inside the pyramid. ☐
3 Three quarters of a million people will live there. ☐
4 Pyramid City will have to withstand tsunamis. ☐

D Read the whole text again and discuss these words:
1 How does the word *futuristic* make you feel? Excited? Scared?
2 *Overcrowding* – what is the first thing that this word makes you think of? Danger?
3 What image do you have of *spider robots*? How big are they? How do they work?

4 TALK ABOUT IT

Which of these ideas do you feel happy with? Evaluate the options that are suggested.
● We have to find accommodation for the populations in our cities. Projects like Sky City are a necessity.
● It would be madness to construct buildings like Pyramid City.
● Sky City will be a safe place in an earthquake.

Cities of the future

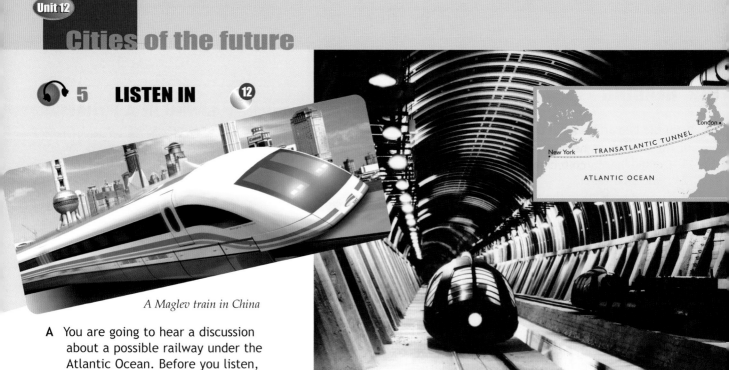

A Maglev train in China

In 1935 a film called Transatlantic Tunnel was made

5 LISTEN IN ⑫

A You are going to hear a discussion about a possible railway under the Atlantic Ocean. Before you listen, match these words with their correct definitions.

1 a magnet is ...	(a) the ability to rise into the air without support
2 levitation is ...	(b) an enclosed space which has no air
3 a vacuum is ...	(c) a piece of metal that attracts other pieces of metal
4 the surface is ...	(d) a heavy object dropped to the bottom of the water to stop a boat moving
5 a section is ...	(e) the top of a body of water (for example a lake, the sea)
6 an anchor is ...	(f) a small part of something larger

B Now match these verbs with their correct definitions.

1 to bend is	(a) to break along a line, but not completely
2 to crack is	(b) to be pushed slowly by the movement of air or water
3 to damage is	(c) to move something so that it is no longer straight
4 to drift is	(d) to harm something (for example a car in an accident)

C Listen to the discussion and answer these questions.
1 What are the two main differences between a magnetically levitated train and a normal train?
2 In which country or countries are there working Maglev trains?
3 What could the top speed of these new trains be?
4 What happens when a normal train reaches a very high speed?
5 What could cause damage to an underwater Maglev train?

6 CONTROVERSY

Work in three teams and discuss the idea of the transatlantic tunnel. Team A thinks it is a waste of money. Team B thinks it may be dangerous. Team C thinks the tunnel is an excellent idea.

SEE ROLE CARDS
FOR UNIT 12

7 PORTFOLIO WRITING

Have you ever played a computer game like SimCity™?
Work in groups to design your ideal city. Make a list of the things your city needs. Then write a report (170 - 200 words) describing your proposed design. Use photos from the internet, if you can.

What my city needs	Type of building	What it looks like
• Accommodation	• High-rise apartments	• A pyramid
• Offices, factories		
• Electricity, water		
• Theatres, museums		
• Transport		

8 DESIGN *in English*

A Before you read the article, discuss these questions.
1 The design of the Bauhaus building was considered revolutionary in 1925. How would you describe it now?
2 Do you think architecture and design are important arts?

Walter Gropius

The Bauhaus in Dessau, Germany

The Bauhaus School began in 1919 in Weimar in Germany. Its teaching influenced art and design throughout the 20th century. In 1933 it was forced to close by the Nazis who considered it too cosmopolitan, and not German enough. Many of its artists and teachers emigrated to the USA.   5
The Bauhaus movement was founded by an architect named Walter Gropius. His aims were to combine art with practical subjects like economics and engineering. For the first time, students were trained by both artists and craftspeople, such as furniture makers. They also learned   10
about science, and developed a new sense of functional design. Designing chairs, lamps and teapots was considered to be as important artistically as painting and sculpture.
Many famous artists were associated with the   15
Bauhaus, for example Paul Klee, Wassily Kandinsky and George Grosz, as well as architects Ludwig Mies van der Rohe and Laszlo Maholy-Nagy, who started a new Bauhaus in Chicago in 1937.

B Read the article and discuss these questions.
1 What were the aims of the Bauhaus movement?
2 How successful do you think the movement was?
3 Why (in your own words) was the Bauhaus closed in 1933?
4 Why do you think so many Bauhaus artists went to America?

9 INTERACTIVE TASK

Work in pairs. Use **Language Bank 21** to help you elicit further ideas and information from your partner.

Student A:	**Student B:**
Choose a controversial remark about modern design as a conversation starter. Choose one that you can continue speaking about. Here are some ideas:	Take control of the conversation by asking questions and making your own controversial remarks. Here are some suggestions:
• Modern architecture is so ugly!	• I think it's great! Why do you think that?
• Today, the design of things like mobile phones is more important than their function.	• Really?... I totally disagree with you on that subject. In fact ...

10 *Your answer:* WHERE WILL WE ALL LIVE?

Having read this unit, discuss these questions with the rest of the class. Here are some suggestions to help you:

A Could you imagine living in Sky City?
• No. It's too high and too crowded.
• Yes! Imagine the view.
B Would it be dangerous to travel in the transatlantic tunnel?
• Yes. Imagine what would happen if terrorists attacked it.
• No. It would be safe and people want to travel faster.
C Do modern designers forget about people?
• Yes. They only want to put more people in a smaller space.
• No. They make everything beautiful and functional.

Unit 13   Call of the wild

What's new?

Subject: National customs
Function: Reporting the conversation of
others; paraphrasing
Grammar: Reported speech

1 *The BIG question:* IS HUNTING A SPORT, A TRADITION OR CRUELTY?

FACT: **Rich tourists take hunting trips to kill lions in Tanzania, elephants in Botswana and bears in Russia.**

Sport hunting for a trophy

Traditional hunting for food

Language: Read these sentences and answer the questions.

- You told me it would be interesting and you were right!
- They said that all the guides spoke English.
- I told the guides that they should change the information in the brochure.
- The guide told him to stop.
- The guide told Curly that he had put all our lives in danger.

A These sentences are all examples of reported speech. In each case, what did the person actually say?

B What is the difference between using **say** and **tell** as the reporting verbs?

C What rules of reported speech can you work out from these sentences?

SEE WORKBOOK UNIT 13

Ideas: The following sentences are from the reading text on the opposite page. Read them and answer the questions.

- A unique opportunity to shoot a huge brown bear, the dream of every real sportsman.
- One of the special pleasures of this hunt is the opportunity to watch bears as they wake up and start roaming around.
- We can't guarantee a kill, but you would be very unlucky to miss out.

A Would you agree that killing a bear was the dream of every real sportsman?

B Is it possible to enjoy watching bears wake up and start roaming around if you intend to shoot them?

C Does the third sentence mean that it is rare or common to succeed in shooting a bear?

2 PREVIEW

Words:

A Look at the photos and answer the questions.
1   What animals are being hunted in the photos? Who are the hunters?
2   Which wild creatures are hunted for sport (**S**) and which are hunted for food (**F**)? Choose from this list:

| bears | deer | wolves | seals | foxes |
| elephants | ducks |

B Why are these and other wild animals hunted?
1   because they are dangerous
2   because there are too many of them
3   for sport
4   because people are cruel
5   for their fur
6   another reason

C Now discuss these questions:
1   Is hunting a national custom in your country?
2   What wild animals are usually hunted?
3   Why do people go hunting?
4   Are there any organisations which are against hunting?
5   What is your personal opinion about hunting and people who hunt?

3 READING

A Before you read Part 1, match the words in **bold** with these definitions.
  1 hot water coming out of the ground
  2 a mass of ice that moves slowly
  3 a mountain that throws out hot gas and rocks

B Read the two texts quickly. Which is:
  1 an article in an environmental magazine?
  2 an advertisement for hunting trips?
  3 an email from someone who has been on a hunting tour?

---

2 QuickMail Pro

Hi Jim!
I just got back from the hunting trip. You told me it would be interesting and you were right!

The trip from New York to Moscow was exhausting! And then we had another long flight from Moscow to the Russian Far East. The brochure said the trip would be short and comfortable – it was neither of those things!

The tour organisers said that Kamchatka bears were the biggest in the world. This is simply not true. They just have European brown bears – nowhere near as big as Alaskan bears! I told the guides that they should change the information in the brochure. They just laughed.

After three days, we came across some bears that were looking for food. One of the other hunters, a big guy called Curly, got a little excited and fired his gun. He missed the bear, and the guide told him to stop. He couldn't speak English so well and Curly looked at him, kind of puzzled. Suddenly, the bear came towards us. Curly got a little scared and fired again. This time he hit and wounded the bear, and it ran off into the forest. The guide told Curly that he had put all our lives in danger. After that, he listened to him.

Anyway, the trip was spectacular. We each shot a bear and we all said we would do it again.

C Explain in your own words these expressions from Part 1.
  1 an untamed place   2 weighs up to 600 kilos
  3 spotted and then stalked

D Answer the questions about these phrases from Part 2.

• You told me it would be interesting ...	1 What was interesting?
• It was neither of those things.	2 What was neither of those things?
• The guide told him to stop.	3 Stop doing what?
• We all said we would do it again.	4 Do what again?

1

HUNT IN RUSSIA
with Kamchatka Hunt Tours

Hunting in Russia is a powerful experience and the most exciting place to hunt is Kamchatka in the Russian Far East. The Kamchatka Peninsula, which is as big as Japan, is separated from Alaska by the Bering Strait. It's an inspiring land of mountains, **volcanoes**, **glaciers** and **hot springs**. It is one of the most exotic, fabulous and untamed places on earth.

Kamchatka gives you a unique opportunity to shoot a huge brown bear, the dream of every real sportsman. A male Kamchatka Brown Bear weighs up to 600kg and can be 2.5 metres long.

Our brown bear hunts last for two weeks. In the early morning, hunters set off with their guides for one of the most exciting hunts of a lifetime! Once a bear is spotted, he is carefully stalked. One of the special pleasures of this hunt is the opportunity to watch bears as they wake up and start roaming around.

There are about seven and a half thousand bears on the peninsula and each hunter is permitted to harvest two. We can't guarantee a kill, but you would be very unlucky to miss out.

The cost is US$7,500 per person.

---

4 TALK ABOUT IT

Two students are reporters. The others are hunters.
A The reporters ask the hunters about the trip they have been on, for example:
  • Why did you want to hunt wild animals like bears?
B The hunters each talk about the trip, for example:
  • It was my dream to hunt bears. I wanted a trophy.
C The reporters then report the hunter's answers to the class, for example:
  • He said that it was his dream to hunt bears.

A tourist bus in Kamchatka

Fish-cleaning competition

Kluchi, an isolated village

 5   LISTEN IN   13

A   You're going to hear part of an illustrated lecture about life on the Kamchatka Peninsula in the Russian Far East. Which of the following things do you expect to hear about?

1   hunting animals for sport   3   fish festivals
2   hunting animals for food   4   tourism

B   Listen and complete the sentences.

1   Kamchatka has a population density of less than one ... per square kilometre.
2   It is not economic to ... the numerous deposits of gold, copper and nickel.
3   Tourism is almost non-existent, and not particularly ....
4   People in Kamchatka depend on the wilderness to ....
5   They hunt brown bears in the spring and then again in the ....
6   Preparing bear meat is a time-consuming ....
7   First the meat must be soaked for 24-36 hours in fresh ....
8   Salmon provide valuable red caviar, which villagers can ....
9   The start of the salmon fishing season is an extremely ... event.
10 There isn't much ... of things to eat because of the short summers.

C   Listen again, and complete these questions and answers.

1   **Q:** What percentage ... Petropavlovsk-Kamchatsky?
    A: About ...
2   **Q:** What mineral deposits are there?
    A: ... , ... and nickel.
3   **Q:** How long ... be soaked?
    A: ...

4   **Q:** What happens ...?
    A: There are ... , wrestling matches and horse races.
5   **Q:** What ... ?
    A: Bread, pink salmon roe ...

6   CONTROVERSY

Have a debate about hunting. Student A is in favour of hunting for sport. Student B is against all forms of hunting. Student C thinks hunting for food is OK.

SEE ROLE CARDS FOR UNIT 13

7   PORTFOLIO WRITING

Write an article (170 - 200 words) about an old national custom, celebration or festival in your country. Imagine that you have asked an older person, a relative or neighbour for example, to describe the customs to you. Your should indicate that you are reporting what he or she said. Use the following guidelines:

Name and time:	*The festival is called ... It happens in Spring/Autumn ...*
History:	*This festival has taken place since ...*
Who told you about it?	*I asked ... about it. He/she is aged ...*
What happens:	*He/she told me that ... He/she said that every ...*

8 CONSTITUTIONAL LAW *in English*

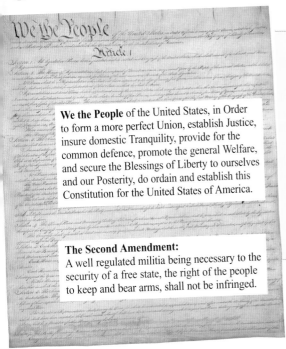

We the People of the United States, in Order to form a more perfect Union, establish Justice, insure domestic Tranquility, provide for the common defence, promote the general Welfare, and secure the Blessings of Liberty to ourselves and our Posterity, do ordain and establish this Constitution for the United States of America.

The Second Amendment:
A well regulated militia being necessary to the security of a free state, the right of the people to keep and bear arms, shall not be infringed.

The right to bear arms

The right to own guns is established in the Second Amendment to the US Bill of Rights, which is itself a series of amendments to the US Constitution. The US Constitution is the supreme law of the United States and the oldest written national constitution in the world. It was completed on September 17th, 1787. It has served as a model for the constitutions of many other nations. The Bill of Rights is the name given to a series of amendments to the Constitution. It is the Second Amendment, proposed in 1789, which is used to defend the rights of US citizens to own and use a weapon.

5

10

A Read the text and answer the questions in your own words:
1 What is the American Constitution?
2 Why do you think that the possession of guns in the USA is so controversial?

B Which of the following is the best explanation of the meaning of the Second Amendment?
1 People should own guns because they may be needed in the army.
2 The only way you can have a good army is to give people the right to have guns.
3 Allowing people to have guns means that the country will be safer and freer.

9 CONVERSATION

In pairs hold a four-minute conversation about one of the photos in this unit, for example:
A The picture above shows the two teenage students who shot 12 other students and a teacher at Columbine High School in Colorado, USA in 1999. Is there a connection between the right to own guns in the USA and this shooting? Start like this:
● Why did they do it, in your opinion?
B The pictures in this Unit show customs in Russia and other countries. Can you describe any similar customs in other places? Use **Language Bank 22** to check you have understood your partner.

The Columbine shooting (CCTV image)

10 *Your answer:* IS HUNTING A SPORT, A TRADITION OR CRUELTY?

Having read this unit, what do you think? Discuss these questions with the rest of the class. Here are some suggestions to help you with the answers:
A Should all hunting be banned?
● Yes, many people think hunting is cruel.
● No. Certain people see hunting as part of their tradition.
B Is it right to condemn hunting when we kill animals for meat?
● At least wild animals have a better life than farm animals.
● By only eating farm animals we can protect wild animals.
C Would we be safer if we banned guns?
● Yes. Many people think we should ban all guns.
● Guns are not dangerous – only the people who use them.

1 *The BIG read*: DUMPED COMPUTERS SOLD ILLEGALLY by Paul Brown

"Only when the last tree is cut; only when the last river is polluted; only when the last fish is caught; only then will they realise that you cannot eat money."   Cree proverb (The Cree are a tribe of Native Americans)

2 PREVIEW

A Work in groups and read the quotation. What does it mean to you? Write a similar warning.

B 1 Read the headline of the newspaper article on the opposite page. What do you think *dumped computers* means?
       (a) computers which have been thrown away
       (b) computers with a virus
   2 *Dumped* is a typical newspaper headline word – short and strong. Think of a less dramatic word or phrase that could be used.

C Read the article quickly and answer the questions about these verbs (underlined in the article).

   1 pose can mean *let someone take a photograph of you*. Does it mean that here?
   2 handle is a noun as well as a verb. Do they mean more or less the same thing?
   3 estimate is a noun as well as a verb: what is the difference in pronunciation between the noun and the verb forms?
   4 arise can mean *get up in the morning*. Does it mean that here?
   5 bother can mean *annoy*. Does it mean that here?

D Check the meaning of these phrases and answer the questions.

| civic amenity site | a place provided by the local authority for recycling of household materials |

1 Are there any civic amenity sites near where you live? What can you take there?

| toxic waste (materials) | things which are thrown away which are poisonous |

2 Have companies ever dumped toxic waste in your country? What kind of waste? Did the companies get into trouble?

| leaded glass | glass which contains lead, which is highly toxic |

3 How and where does lead cause pollution problems?

3 READING

A Read the article. Find these words and expressions in **bold** in the text. Try to work out the meaning from the context.

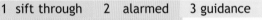

1 sift through	2 alarmed	3 guidance
4 injustice	5 cannibalised	
6 working models	7 grey area	8 discarded

B Now read the article carefully and answer these questions. Use your own words — don't quote directly from the text.
   1 How are computers recycled?
   2 Why did the work of totters become illegal?
   3 How many computer monitors are being sent to the developing world?
   4 Does the new law suggest that all old computers are toxic waste?
   5 Why don't people in the UK bother to fix some of the equipment?

4 TALK ABOUT IT

Work in groups.
   1 Make a list of domestic electrical items which are likely to be discarded.
   2 Think of imaginative uses for these items when they are recycled.
   3 Present your list and ideas to the rest of the class.

5 PORTFOLIO WRITING

A Write a summary of the article in about 200 words.
B Write an article (170 - 200 words) suggesting how other products, such as cars, could be recycled.

⑮

Dumped computers and TV sets sold illegally to developing world

① Millions of television sets and old computer monitors taken to civic amenity sites as rubbish are being collected and shipped to Africa and Asia, an illegal trade worth £7m a 5 year, according to an unpublished report by the Environment Agency and the recycling industry. The business carried out by totters – people who **sift through** rubbish 10 for saleable objects – became illegal on the 1st of January 2002 under European Union legislation designed to prevent toxic waste materials being shipped to developing 15 countries.

② Electrical equipment containing leaded glass, particularly computers and televisions, were reclassified as toxic waste because of the danger 20 lead <u>poses</u> to people <u>handling</u> the equipment or breaking it up. The agency is **alarmed** that half a million televisions and a similar number of computer monitors which people 25 thought were being disposed of in England are being re-used or dumped in the developing world.

③ The agency is finding the trade hard to control but is planning to 30 publish **guidance** to the industry soon. Environment groups say that will not be sufficient to stop an illegal business.

④ Claire Wilton of Friends of the Earth 35 said: "The agency has known about this situation for two years but has still failed to act. The companies involved in this illegal trade must be prevented from dumping Britain's 40 toxic waste on developing countries, where workers' conditions rarely match those expected in Europe. "Action must be taken now to stop this environmental **injustice** continuing." 45

⑤ The Industry Council for Electronic Equipment Recycling (ICER) <u>estimates</u> that 11,000 tonnes of old TV sets, about 500,000 in total, and a similar number of old computer monitors 50 find their way to developing countries each year. Many are **cannibalised** for spare parts but some are repaired and sold to people who would not otherwise have a television or 55 computer.

⑥ ICER defends its members who buy computers and other office equipment from industry and ship them abroad, because under EU 60 rules the business is legal if they are **working models** and intended to be sold on the second-hand market. The problem <u>arises</u> when equipment is thrown away. The law says if it is 65 discarded, even if it may be working, it must be classed as rubbish and cannot be resold to a developing country because it is technically toxic waste. 70

⑦ The report, completed three months ago, says the problem is that totters and other small businesses which collect old TVs and computers sell them on to bulk 75 dealers unaware of the final destination. "Ultimate destinations of equipment include Eastern Europe, the Far East, the Indian sub-continent, West Africa and China. 80 Some take the view that the re-use of unwanted goods is desirable. "There is a **grey area** here about some of the exports," said Claire Snow of ICER. "Are they second- 85 hand goods in working order and therefore legal, or discarded and in need of repair, and illegal? One of the problems is that something that needs fixing but is too expensive to 90 <u>bother</u> with in the UK because of labour costs becomes economic in the developing world. If they can get use out of it, some reason that it is not a bad thing to export." 95

⑧ The Environment Agency says that if something has been **discarded**, even if it can be used again, it is illegal to export it to a developing country.

By Paul Brown, Environment Correspondent, *The Guardian*

What's new?

Subject:	Dreams and nightmares
Function:	Expressing abstract ideas
Grammar:	Passives with modals (*can be seen, should be read*)

1 **The BIG question:** WHY IS FANTASY SO POPULAR?

 FACT: More than 300 million copies of the Harry Potter fantasy stories have been sold in 200 countries.

Three types of fantasy

2 PREVIEW

Words:

A Match the sentences with the explanations of the word *fantasy*.

1	I enjoy reading fantasy novels.	(a)	not seeing life as it really is.
2	She has a fantasy about being a star.	(b)	stories that are very different from everyday life.
3	He confuses fantasy with reality.	(c)	a pleasant experience that you imagine.

B Look at the pictures and answer these questions.
   1 What do the pictures have in common?
   2 Have you read the books, seen the shows or the films? Did you like them?

C Work in pairs. Underline the statements you agree with.

1	Fantasy is:	(a) an escape from the real world for dreamers.
		(b) a change from the real world for everyone.
2	Fantasy films are:	(a) imaginative and exciting.
		(b) boring and unrealistic.
3	Fantasy books are:	(a) a clever way to explore new ideas.
		(b) an easy way to avoid real life.

D Describe these creatures from fantasy literature, for example:
● a wizard is old, and has long silver hair and a long silver beard.

witch	wizard	dragon	fairy
prince/princess		vampire	

Language: Read these sentences:
● It **can be seen** as a predecessor to the Harry Potter novels.
● This is something that **must never be done**.
● This book **should be read** by all.

A Are these sentences active or passive?
B Do they refer to the past or present?
C What do the words in **bold** have in common?

 <u>SEE WORKBOOK UNIT 14</u>

Ideas: The following sentences are from the reading text on the opposite page. Read them and answer the questions.
● The words of the enchantment hissed on Ged's lips, and he cried out, "Elfarran!"
● A pale oval of light gleamed between his opened arms. In this light for a moment there moved a form, a human shape.
● And through the bright breach climbed something like a lump of black shadow, and it leapt straight out at Ged's face.

A Ged, a boy wizard, has cast a spell. What happens next that is frightening?
B Do these sentences make you want to read the rest of the text? Say why / why not.

3   READING

BOOK REVIEW:

First published in 1968, this is the first book in *The Earthsea Trilogy*. It tells the story of Ged, a boy who goes to wizard school. It can be seen as a predecessor to the Harry Potter novels, in which Harry also goes to a school for wizards. Ged is arrogant and calls up a spirit from the dead. This is something that must never be done, as it is against all the laws of nature. Out of a 'rip' in the 'fabric' of the world, a terrifying shadow climbs... This book should be read by all who enjoy fantasy literature.

16 *A Wizard of Earthsea*
by Ursula K. Le Guin

The other boys stood watching, not speaking, not moving unless they shivered a little; for the great spell was beginning to work. Ged's voice was soft still, but changed, with a deep singing in it, and the words he spoke were not known to them. He fell silent. Suddenly the wind rose roaring in the grass. Ged dropped to his knees and called out aloud. Then he fell forward as if to embrace the earth with his outstretched arms, and when he rose he held something dark in his hands and arms, something so heavy that he shook with effort getting to his feet. The hot wind whined in the black grasses on the hill. If the stars shone now, none saw them.

The words of the enchantment hissed on Ged's lips, and then he cried out aloud and clearly, "Elfarran!" Again he cried the name, "Elfarran!" And the third time, "Elfarran!"

The shapeless mass of darkness he had lifted split apart. A pale oval of light gleamed between his opened arms, reaching from the ground up to the height of his raised hands. In this light for a moment there moved a form, a human shape: a tall woman looking back over her shoulder. Her face was beautiful, and sorrowful, and full of fear.

Only for a moment did the spirit glimmer there. Then the oval between Ged's arms grew bright. It widened and

spread, a ripping open of the fabric of the world. Through it blazed a terrible brightness. And through the bright breach climbed something like a lump of black shadow, quick and ugly, and it leaped straight out at Ged's face.

Staggering back under the weight of the thing, Ged gave a short scream. Ged fell, struggling and writhing, while the bright rip in the world's darkness above him widened and stretched. The boys that watched fled, and Jasper bent down to the ground hiding his eyes from the terrible light. Vetch alone ran forward to his friend. So only he saw the lump of shadow that clung to Ged, tearing at his flesh. It was like a black beast, the size of a young child, though it seemed to grow and shrink; and it had no head and face, only the four paws with which it gripped and tore. Vetch sobbed with horror, yet he put out his hands to try to pull the thing away from Ged. Before he touched it, he was bound still, unable to move.

The intolerable brightness faded, and slowly the torn edges of the world closed together. Nearby a voice was speaking as softly as a tree whispers or a fountain plays. Starlight began to shine again, and the grasses of the hillside were whitened with the light of the moon just rising. The night was healed.

A Wizard of Earthsea, by Ursula K. le Guin,
published by Puffin Books

A Scan the whole text quickly. Give brief answers to these questions.
1   Who is Vetch? What does he try to do?
2   What happens to the 'bright rip in the world's darkness' at the end of the extract?

B Read the Book Review carefully. Say if these sentences are true (**T**) or false (**F**).   T/F
1   *A Wizard of Earthsea* is similar in one way to the Harry Potter novels. ☐
2   Ged's spell follows the laws of nature. ☐

C Read the extract carefully.
1   How is the spirit that Ged calls up described?
2   What does Jasper do?
3   Why do you think Vetch is unable to move?

4   TALK ABOUT IT

A Ged has released 'a lump of black shadow'. How do you think his life changes as a result?

B Work in pairs. Write a paragraph that continues the story. Then show your paragraph to another pair, who read it and say how the paragraph can be improved or corrected.
Examples:
●   Your paragraph's great, but there are ways that it can be improved.
●   We suggest that the first sentence should be changed / rewritten like this: ...

🎧 **5   LISTEN IN** 🔵14

(a) Brad Pitt in Interview with a Vampire

(b) Tom Cruise in Mission Impossible 2

A Look at the photos.
1 Which photo is from a horror film and which is from a thriller?
2 Explain the difference.

B Which of these words (abstract nouns) could be used in a discussion about:
1 a horror film   2 a comedy   3 a thriller

(a) terror	(b) suspense	(c) fear	(d) violence
(e) horror	(e) amusement	(f) entertainment	(g) excitement

C What adjectives can be formed from these abstract nouns?

1 terror	2 violence	3 fear	4 horror	5 excitement
(a) terrifying	(b)	(c)	(d)	(e)

D Listen and complete the sentences.
1 The first speaker, Dave, says that he ... for the horror movie.
2 Nancy says that she hates ....
3 Tom says that the film they plan to watch is meant to be one of the best ... movies ever made.
4 Nancy described the two male speakers as a ....
5 During the film, Tom says that the ... is killing him.
6 Dave thinks the film is ... at its best.
7 Nancy thinks the film will give them bad ....
8 Tom notices that the ... is on next week.

E Listen again. What are the differences between these sentences and the words in the audio? Say if they change the meaning.
1 The idea of witches and vampires frightens me.
2 I'm getting some drinks.
3 That was entertainment at its worst.
4 It'll be a relief when it's over.
5 You don't like horror movies.

6   CONTROVERSY

Work in pairs. Student A wants to watch a horror movie on video. Student B prefers a fantasy film.

📇 SEE ROLE CARDS FOR UNIT 14

7   PORTFOLIO WRITING

Write a film review for a magazine (170 - 200 words).

Introduction: Basic information
• *(name of film)* is a new comedy/ thriller/ drama ...
• ... *directed* by *(name of director)*.
• ... starring *(names of main actors)* ... as ... *(name of character)*
• ... with *(name of actor)* in the role of ...

Paragraph 1: The story (in the present tense):
• The story takes place in ...
• It's about ... It describes/shows the ...

Paragraph 2: Giving your opinion
• The photography/acting is ...
• *(Name of actor)* is not very ...
• I found the film rather ...

Conclusion:
• This film should not be missed.

8 LITERATURE in English

A Before you read, look at the picture. Say what you know about the story.

MARY SHELLEY AND FRANKENSTEIN

In 1816, an eighteen-year-old English girl called Mary Shelley was staying in a villa by Lake Geneva in Switzerland with her husband, the young poet Percy Bysshe Shelley. With them was Mary's half sister and another poet, Lord Byron, who was already famous. That weekend the young people were speculating on the newly discovered power of electricity. This gave them the idea that each should write a ghost story. That night, unable to sleep, Mary had a vision that she described in her journal: "I saw, with shut eyes, a pale student kneeling beside the thing he had put together. An engine clanked and the monster showed signs of life and stirred. Horror-stricken, the student rushed away ... He hoped that the spark of life he had given the creature would fade and the creature would become lifeless once more .... The student slept. But when he woke, the horrid thing was at his bedside, opening his curtains and looking at him with yellow, watery, wondering eyes." Mary realised that, "what terrified me will terrify others – I need only describe the ghost that haunted my midnight vision." She began writing the next day, and her novel, *Frankenstein*, was published early in 1818. The story has remained popular till this day. It is probably the most well-known example of the Gothic fiction genre that was popular at the time. Gothic novels involved the fantastic and supernatural, and were full of suspense and mystery. *Frankenstein* can be described as the first great horror story.

Boris Karloff as the monster from the 1931 film, Frankenstein

B Read the passage above. Explain in your own words:
1 What was unusual about Mary Shelley as an author.
2 How Mary got the idea for her story.
3 In what way the Gothic genre is similar to a modern horror story.

C Work in small groups. Discuss why *Frankenstein* is still popular today.

9 CONVERSATION

A In pairs, using the examples below, hold a five-minute conversation about a story or novel that could be turned into a good film. Take turns and use **Language Bank 23** to add abstract ideas.
- *Space Wars* could be made into a good film.
- It would be terrifying, but dramatic.
- I don't agree. It would be too violent and horrifying!
- It would be a thriller. Imagine being lost in space.

B In pairs, discuss a film you would like to make, for example:
- A typical day at college could be made into a comedy.
- Our teacher must be played by Brad Pitt.

10 Your answer: WHY IS FANTASY SO POPULAR?

Having read this unit, what do you think? Discuss these questions with the rest of the class. Here are some suggestions to help you with the answers.
A What's so good about fantasy?
- People enjoy escaping from everyday life.
- It's very exciting and imaginative.
B Do you enjoy fantasy?
- No, I don't. It's too unrealistic.
- Yes, I love to dream about ...
C How do you feel about horror films?
- They're too scary and violent.
- I love the suspense.

Think big!

What's new?

Subject: The world of work
Function: Expressing likes and dislikes
Grammar: Verbs + *-ing* or an infinitive

1 *The BIG question:* WOULD YOU LIKE TO MAKE A MILLION?

FACT: The most trusted professionals are nurses, pharmacists, vets, doctors and teachers. The best-paid professionals are soccer players, racing drivers and people who work in legal and financial services.

2 PREVIEW

Words:

A Can you identify the professions of the people in these photos? Choose from the words in the FACT box.

B 1 Which of the people in the FACT box help others?
   2 Which of them do you think do the most important work?
   3 Would you like to do any of these jobs?

C Explain the differences between these pairs of words or phrases:

   1 part-time job / full-time job
   2 entrepreneur / executive
   3 an experience / experience (abstract noun)
   4 legal services / financial services

D Decide if you think these sentences are true (**T**) or false (**F**).   **T / F**
   1 It's impossible to be a student and have a full-time job. ☐
   2 Professionals are highly trained; workers are less well-trained. ☐
   3 An entrepreneur usually likes working for him or herself. ☐

Language: Read these sentences and answer the questions.

- I didn't plan to do this because I don't enjoy working for other people.
- I aimed to provide computer editing services.
- My advice to young people who consider starting a company is always the same.
- Do it now! Don't delay starting it until you've finished business school.

A What is the difference between the way we use these two lists of verbs?

| 1 | ● plan | ● aim | ● hope | ● decide |
| 2 | ● enjoy | ● consider | ● delay | ● imagine |

B Can you think of three other verbs like the verbs in list 1?
C And three other verbs like those in list 2?

SEE WORKBOOK UNIT 15

Ideas: The following sentences are from the reading text on the opposite page. Read them and answer the questions.
- Most students in America take part-time jobs.
- I started my own company.
- If you hope to be financially independent, you must do something while you are young.

A Have you ever had a part-time job? If so, describe it.
B How do you feel about starting your own company?
C Would you like to work for yourself?

3 READING

A You are going to read an article about a student who made a million dollars. Five sentences have been removed from the text. Choose from the sentences (A)-(E) the one which fits each gap (1)-(4). There is one extra sentence which you do not need to use.

(A) I didn't plan to do this because I don't enjoy working for other people.
(B) I like working for other people, so I gave up plans to start my own company.
(C) Don't delay starting it until you've finished business school or had some 'real-world experience'.
(D) After the article appeared in March, interested investors began emailing me.
(E) Then I hired my first four employees, and I never edited a single document again.

Editing students' essays

HOW STUDENT GEOFF COOK MADE A MILLION

1 Most students in America take part-time jobs to help to pay for their studies. (1) .... I started my own company, CyberEdit, when I was 19. Most students have to write essays, and I aimed to provide computer editing services for them. It was an instant success. During one summer vacation, I worked for an internet company and in the evening, I spent another four hours working on my website. After that summer, my company grew by about 400%, earning me $40,000 in the first year.

2 It's not easy to develop a business. If you hope to be financially independent, you must do something while you are young and you can work long hours. For a long time, I was editing between five and ten documents a night, I spent fifty hours a week doing this. It was hard – I was taking some difficult maths courses at the same time. (2) ....

3 The next year, I turned down a summer job at a big New York investment bank and spent the vacation expanding CyberEdit. In December, *Wired* magazine contacted me and asked me to write an article about my life. (3) .... In June, one of the people who had emailed me decided to invest a large sum of money in the company. So... the *Wired* article brought me over a million dollars in funding!

4 More than anything else, good publicity helps a new business attract investors and customers. A successful teenage entrepreneur is an interesting story, so getting publicity and funding for the business was easier because of my age. Investors came to me, not because I was making money and employing fifty people from college, but because they read about it in *Wired* magazine, and saw it on *ABC World News Tonight*.

5 My advice to young people who consider starting a company is always the same: Do it now! (4) .... In college and high school, you have the benefit of youth. You're in an environment that's focused on work, with a place to live and plenty of fast-food options. In a way, combining college and entrepreneurship was the smartest thing I've ever done.

B Skim paragraph 1 and find out what kind of business Geoff Cook started.

C Read paragraph 2 and decide if these sentences are true (**T**) or false (**F**):

	T / F
1 In the company's first year, Geoff did all the work himself.	☐
2 Geoff spent 50 hours a week studying math.	☐

D Read paragraphs 3 and 4 and answer these questions:
1 What happened as a result of the article in *Wired* magazine?
2 Why is it good to start a business when you are young?

E Read paragraph 5 and find words which mean:
1 advantage   2 thinking about
3 doing two different things at the same time

4 TALK ABOUT IT

Work in pairs and discuss these questions. Use **Language Bank 24** to discuss questions A and B.

A Would you like to start your own company? Say why / why not.
B What kind of work do you enjoy? What work do you dislike?
c What do you think about students having professional help with essays?

5 LISTEN IN

A Imagine you were being interviewed for this job. Answer these questions:
1 Why would you like to work for our organisation?
2 What special qualities do you have that would be useful to us?

PROJECT ENGINEERS FOR HOSPITAL IN INDIA

Medical Services Organisation requires engineers for new hospital project in India. Apply with CV to HR Dept, Hall International, London.

B You're going to listen to two different interviews for the same job. Before you listen, answer the following questions:
1 What does *the successful candidate* mean?
2 Is it good or bad if you graduate with a first-class degree? Why?
3 What does the Human Resources Department of a company do?
4 What's the difference between the *developed world* and the *developing world*?

C Listen to the interviews and answer Yes or No. Then give details.

	Yes/No
1 Is the first candidate really interested in the work?	☐
2 Does the first interviewer give any details about the job?	☐
3 Has the second candidate done any research for the interview?	☐
4 Does the second interviewer think much of the candidate's qualifications?	☐

D What is your opinion of the attitude and behaviour of:
1 the first interviewer?
2 the first candidate?
3 the second interviewer?
4 the second candidate?

6 CONTROVERSY

In groups of four, write a job advertisement. Hold interviews for the job. Two of you are interviewers. The other two are candidates. Who gets the job?

 SEE ROLE CARDS FOR UNIT 15

Explaining why you would like the job

7 PORTFOLIO WRITING

Write a letter or email to apply for a part-time job working with a British or American company in a business that interests you. Include information about your qualifications, your level of English and what you already know about the company (120–150 words).

Begin:	Dear Sir/Madam,
Introduction:	I would like to apply for the position advertised in …
Qualifications	I have a university degree in …
Level of English:	I have passed the Trinity College London Grade 9.
End:	I look forward to hearing from you shortly. Yours faithfully,
Your name:	

8 *BUSINESS in English*

A Which of these jobs are in service industries (**S**) and which are in manufacturing (**M**) industries?

1 Auto engineering ☐   2 Paper-making ☐
3 Women's fashion ☐   4 Tourism ☐

B Now make two lists of other jobs in manufacturing and services.

C 1 Look at the graph. Decide if these sentences are true (**T**) or false (**F**):

T / F

(a) There are now fewer manufacturing jobs for both men and women. ☐

(b) There are more service industry jobs for men than for women. ☐

2 Has the world of work changed in your country in the same way as it has in Britain?

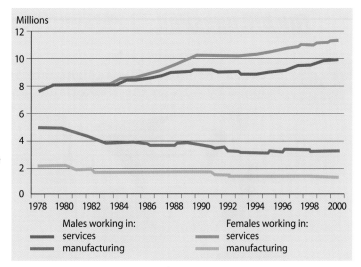

UK: More service industries, less manufacturing

---

1 ....?
Financial and business services now [1] account for about one in five jobs in the UK, compared with about one in ten in 1981. This shows that in Britain there has been a dramatic [5] growth in the service industries and a big decline in manufacturing industries over the last 25 years.

2 ....?
There has also been an increase in the number of jobs for women. [10] Today, the numbers of men and women working are almost equal, although almost half of women work part-time. Men are still paid more. Women's average income is [15] only 81% of men's.

3 ....?
More than 10% of all working people now work for themselves. Men are more likely than women to work for themselves – 73% of the three million [20] self-employed people are male. People from certain ethnic groups, Asians for example, are more likely to be self-employed than others.

D Read the text quickly. Which of these questions goes with each of the paragraphs above?

- Are more women working than men?
- Have the types of jobs in Britain changed?
- Who is more likely to be self-employed?

9 YOUR TOPIC

Work in pairs. Prepare a four-minute presentation on a subject connected with work, for example what it's like to be self-employed. Student A: Make notes of the main points. Introduce your topic:

- I'm going to discuss self-employment.

Be prepared to answer questions, and give examples and explanations.
Student B: Ask relevant questions and ask for clarification when you don't understand. (**Language Bank 5**)

10 *Your answer:* WOULD YOU LIKE TO MAKE A MILLION?

Having read this unit, what do you think? Discuss these questions with the rest of the class. Here are some suggestions to help you.

A Would you like to make a million dollars?
- Yes, my ambition is to make a lot of money.
- No, I'm more interested in work which helps other people.

B How important is money to you?
- I consider that it's important to like your job.
- I don't think that money can make you happy.
- I plan to make money and then enjoy myself.

C What would your ideal job be?
- I'd love to be a really successful musician.
- I'd enjoy working as a doctor.

Unit 16 # Throw away the key

What's new?

Subject:	Crime and punishment
Function:	Expressing regrets
Grammar:	Third conditional; past use of *wish*

1 *The BIG question:* IS PRISON THE BEST WAY TO STOP CRIME?

FACT: Between the late 1970s and the late 1990s, deaths from the use of heroin dropped by 40% in the Netherlands and tripled in the US.

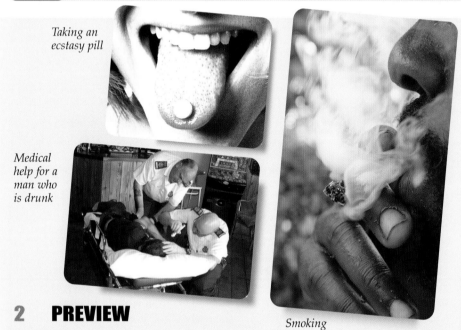

Taking an ecstasy pill

Medical help for a man who is drunk

Smoking

Language: Read these sentences and answer the questions.
- I wish the Americans would stop blaming us for their social problems.
- We wish they had thought about this more carefully, but clearly they didn't.

A Which of the above sentences refers to now and which refers to the past?
- If Mr Walters had checked the facts more carefully, he would have seen that we have made an enormous effort to improve the situation.

B Does the sentence above refer to the past or the present?

C Does the speaker think that Mr Walters checked his facts?

SEE WORKBOOK UNIT 16

2 PREVIEW

Words:

A Match the expressions with their definitions:

1	hard drugs	(a)	drugs used by groups of friends in some countries
2	soft drugs	(b)	dangerous drugs which are illegal in most countries
3	social drugs	(c)	less strong drugs which are illegal in most countries

B Look at the list and answer the questions.

(a) marijuana	(b) ecstasy	(c) amphetamine
(d) heroin	(e) cocaine	(f) tobacco
(g) caffeine	(h) alcohol	

1 Which of these would you call a drug?
2 Number them (1–8) according to how dangerous you think they are.
3 Which of them are illegal in your country?

C Put the drugs in B into the correct category.

Hard drugs	Soft drugs	Social drugs

Ideas: The following sentences are from the reading text on the opposite page. Read them and answer the questions.
- He thinks that many European governments are too soft on the use of recreational drugs.
- Many European countries have a policy of therapy instead of punishment for possession of drugs.
- The government is spending 150 million yuan to build drug rehabilitation centres.

A What is an example of *soft* punishment?

B What is the difference between *therapy* and *punishment*?

C What do you think a *rehabilitation centre* is?

3 READING

A Read the two texts quickly and find out who these people are.

| 1 John Walters | 2 Martin Witteveen | 3 Yu Zhuoxiong | 4 Xie Fuxing |

1 US Drug Controller blasts Dutch drug policy

John Walters is the director of the US Office of National Drug Control Policy and he isn't a happy man. He thinks that many European governments are too soft on the use of recreational drugs such as marijuana.

His main criticism is directed against the Netherlands, where he claims that laboratories are manufacturing tons of drugs, including ecstasy, which end up in the United States.

"Some European governments think it's OK to tolerate the use of drugs," said Walters. "We wish they had thought about this more carefully, but clearly they didn't. This is a fundamentally irrational health policy and social policy," he added. He believes that the policies have led to the creation of a new generation of drug addicts.

Many European countries have a policy of therapy instead of punishment for possession of drugs for personal use. Prison is a last resort for the punishment of drug users.

In the Netherlands, the police are not so concerned with soft drugs, such as marijuana. Nowadays, they concentrate on stopping the manufacture and sale of hard drugs, such as heroin and cocaine.

Martin Witteveen is a Dutch prosecutor for drug crimes and he thinks that the US criticism is not justified. "I wish the Americans would stop blaming us for their social problems," he said. "If Mr Walters had checked the facts more carefully, he would have seen that we have made an enormous effort to improve the situation."

The Netherlands: sign outside a shop

China: Drug traffickers sentenced to death

2 Death penalty for drug dealers

A court sentenced three drug traffickers to death on Friday in Guangzhou, capital of South China's Guangdong Province.

Yu Zhuoxiong and two other members of his gang were convicted of selling and trafficking more than 200 kilos of methamphetamine, a drug known as ice. Six other members of the gang were sentenced to life in jail.

Yu and his gang produced and sold, among other things, more than 4 million ecstasy pills, 3,000 kilograms of ice and 800 kilograms of caffeine. South Africa was the main market for most of the drugs.

"I hope that this trial will mean that the drug problem in this city has ended," said Xie Fuxing, vice-director of Guangzhou City Public Security Bureau. The Guangdong provincial government is spending 150 million yuan (18.3 million US dollars) to build drug rehabilitation centres with a total of 16,000 beds to accommodate drug addicts for treatment.

B Find these sentences in Text 1 and answer the questions.
- Prison is a last resort for the punishment of drug users.
1 Does this mean that prison is like a holiday for drug users?
- ... the US criticism is not justified.
2 Does this mean that the criticism is unlawful?

C Find these words in Text 2.

| (a) sentenced | (b) convicted | (c) trafficking |

1 What do they mean?
2 In what phrases do they usually appear?
3 Can you use the words in different contexts?

D Now read the two texts more carefully and answer using your own words.
1 What are John Walters' main criticisms of the Dutch policy?
2 What did the Chinese gang produce and where was it used?
3 What is the government doing to solve the drug problem in Guangzhou?

4 TALK ABOUT IT

A Work in groups. Discuss the following questions.

1 Is your country's attitude to the use of drugs more similar to the Netherlands or to China?
2 Do you think that the death penalty is a suitable punishment for drug trafficking?

B Work in pairs.
Student A: you are a gang member in jail for life for drug trafficking. Talk about your regrets. Use **Language Bank 25**.
Student B: You are visiting your friend in jail.

Unit 16

Throw away the key

5 LISTEN IN

A You are going to hear a radio broadcast about the controversial Three-Strikes Law in California. Before you listen, read the following facts about it:
- The law was designed to reduce violent crime.
- People who offend three times go to prison for life.
- It doesn't matter if the three crimes were violent or not.

B Listen to the broadcast and underline the correct definition for each phrase.

1	on parole	(a) someone is in prison	(b) someone is out of prison
2	repeat offender	(a) someone has committed more than one crime	(b) someone has committed the same crime twice
3	law came into force	(a) the law was very strong	(b) the law became official
4	victim of crime	(a) someone who helps to commit a crime	(b) someone who has been harmed by a criminal
5	the wrong people put away	(a) the wrong people go to prison	(b) the wrong people avoid going to prison

C Tick ✔ the box if the person holds this opinion. Put a cross ✘ if the person definitely does NOT hold the opinion.

Opinion	Carl Brewer	Kelly McGuire
1 I'm in favour of the Three-Strikes Law.		
2 I'm in favour of long prison sentences for violent people.		
3 The majority of Three-Strikes offenders have committed non-violent crimes.		
4 Violent crime has decreased since the law was introduced.		

D Survey everyone in the class about these opinions. Work out the opinion of the class as percentages.

Criminals should go to prison for life:	Yes	No	Don't know
1 only after committing three violent crimes.			
2 after committing three crimes, violent or not.			

Where does the idea of three strikes come from?

6 CONTROVERSY

Work in groups of four. Hold a debate, supporting or opposing this motion:
- We believe that the Three-Strikes Law should be introduced in our country.

SEE ROLE CARDS FOR UNIT 16

7 PORTFOLIO WRITING

Diary of a life prisoner

Thursday 18th: Exactly the same as any other day. Breakfast at 6am, the usual tasteless rubbish. I was forced to stay in my cell until lunch time. One hour of recreation. I walked round the prison yard, but I wasn't allowed to talk to anyone. My prison rights have been taken away. I had a fight with another prisoner. If I hadn't hit him, he would have continued to say offensive things about me.

Imagine the prisoner is released early. Write his diary for his first day of freedom (170 - 200 words). Add some regrets about the time he spent in prison. Use **Language Bank 25** for expressions indicating regret.

74

8 HUMAN RIGHTS in English

A Look at the pictures and answer these questions.
1   Have you heard of the Universal Declaration of Human Rights?
2   Do you know any of what the Declaration says?

The Universal Declaration of Human Rights

On December 10th, 1948, the General Assembly of the United Nations adopted the Universal Declaration of Human Rights. In part, it was in response to the atrocities of World War II. The Declaration has been translated into more than 300 languages, from Abkhaz to Zulu. There are thirty articles in the Declaration. Here is a summary of the first five:

Article 1: All human beings are born free and equal.
Article 2: Everyone is entitled to all the rights and freedoms in this Declaration, without distinction of any kind, such as race, colour, sex, language, religion, political or other opinion, national or social origin, property, birth or other status.
Article 3: Everyone has the right to life, liberty and security of person.
Article 4: No one shall be held in slavery or servitude.
Article 5: No one shall be subjected to torture or to cruel, inhuman or degrading treatment or punishment.

An artist's image of Article 5. Do you think it is an accurate image? Why? Why not?

Eleanor Roosevelt helped to write the Declaration

B Read the text and find words and expressions that mean the following
1   a short account of something which gives the main information
2   another word for *freedom*
3   extreme cruelty

C Work in groups. Study each of the articles and answer the questions.
1   Do all people everywhere have all these rights?
2   Do you know places where people do not have some of these rights?

9 INTERACTIVE TASK

Hold a four-minute conversation:
Student A: Make notes and begin talking about:
•   What is the most important human right of all?
Student B: Take control of the conversation and respectfully ask questions.
See **Language Bank 26.**

10 Your answer: IS PRISON THE BEST WAY TO STOP CRIME?

Having read this unit, what do you think? Discuss these questions with the rest of the class. Here are some suggestions to help you.
A   Should all drug users be sent to prison?
•   Yes, because all drugs are dangerous.
•   People who are addicted to drugs are ill and need treatment.
B   Does the idea of prison stop people trying drugs?
•   It stops some people, but not others.
C   What kind of thing do you think drug users regret?
•   If I hadn't taken soft drugs, I wouldn't have gone on to hard drugs.

Unit 17 — Surviving disaster

What's new?

Subject:	Risk and adventure
Function:	Evaluating past actions/course of events
Grammar:	*should/could* + present perfect

1 *The BIG question:* ARE YOU A SURVIVOR?

FACT: More than 1,400 people have climbed Mount Everest. More than 170 of them died, about one in eight.

2 PREVIEW

Mountaineer on Mount Everest

Famous climber Lynn Hill

Hiker in the wilderness

Words:

A Look up the meaning of these words and answer the questions.

mountaineer	hiker	boulder	climber
to survive	canyon	search	rescue

1 Which of these words describe people who visit the wilderness?
2 Which of these words describe parts of the wilderness?
3 Which of these words are connected to disasters?

B 1 What's the difference in meaning between these pairs of nouns?
   (a) survival / survivor   (b) rescue / rescuer
2 Tick ✓ the combinations of words that are correct.
   (a) to make risks ☐   (c) to set off ☐
   (b) to take risks ☐   (d) to set out ☐

Language: Read these sentences and answer the questions.

- There are a lot of things he should have done.
- He shouldn't have set off without doing at least one of these things.
- He could have taken a cell phone with him.
- He could have asked someone to do the hike with him.

A 1 Read the first sentence. Did he do these things or not? **Yes/No**
2 Read the second sentence. Did he set off or not? **Yes/No**

B In the first and second sentences, what does the speaker mean by *should have* and *shouldn't have*? More than one answer may be correct.
1 The action referred to took place in the past.
2 He/she recommends another action.
3 He/she doesn't think what the person did was right.

C In the third and fourth sentences, what do the words *could have* indicate?
1 Something which possibly happened
2 A possible choice of action
3 Something that someone used to do

 SEE WORKBOOK UNIT 17

Ideas: The following sentences are from the reading text on the opposite page. Read them and then answer the questions.
- He expected the hike would take him about 12 hours.
- Ralston had broken the most important rule of climbing.
- The media made him into a hero.

A Does the first sentence mean that he *hoped* the hike would take that long?
B Can you imagine what *the most important rule of climbing* is?
C Does sentence 3 mean that he wouldn't have been a hero if his story hadn't appeared in the newspapers and on TV?

3   READING

A Scan the title and the first two paragraphs of the article. Summarise the story in your own words.

B Before you read the article in detail, check the meaning of these expressions.
1   Is a *stable frame of mind* a good thing for: (a) an airline pilot   (b) an artist?
2   Does *to keep your head* mean: (a) to be calm   (b) to shout loudly?
3   Does the *wilderness experience* mean: (a) the feeling of adventure   (b) the skill of surviving?

DID CLIMBER HAVE TO CUT OFF ARM TO SAVE LIFE?

Cliff Ransom
National Geographic Adventure magazine

On Sunday the 27th April 2003, 27-year-old Aron Ralston, an experienced mountaineer, set off on a 13-mile (21 km) hike through the Bluejohn Canyon in Utah. He expected the hike would take him about 12 hours. On his way, while climbing through a narrow section of the canyon, an 800-pound (360 kg) boulder fell and trapped his arm. He was unable to move.

Ralston lay trapped in the canyon for five days. His water ran out after four days. A search party that went looking for him found no sign of him. On Thursday, he used a pocket knife to amputate his arm below the elbow. He then walked out of the canyon and was taken to hospital.

Search and rescue veteran Rex Tanner was asked what Ralston did right and wrong.

How do you think Ralston managed to survive?
Rex: I think the most important thing is that he kept his head. In an emergency situation, you need a stable frame of mind.

What could Ralston have done to avoid the situation?
Rex: Ralston had broken the most important rule of climbing. He had not told anyone where he was going. There are a lot of things he should have done that he didn't do. For example, he could have asked someone to do the hike with him. He could have taken a cell phone with him. He shouldn't have set out without doing at least one of these things. It's really not that difficult to do, and it doesn't take away from the wilderness experience.

Ralston's story was broadcast from England to Brazil. What do you think about that?
Rex: The media made him into a hero. But they never talked about how the guy got himself into trouble because he made some bad decisions. When someone gets himself into trouble, the lives of the people who are trying to help him may be in danger. He should have thought about that.

What basic tips would you suggest to help people survive in the wild?
Rex: Having enough water is number one. Being able to start a fire is number two. The proper clothing is important. Also, you have to realize when things are getting difficult. Before you climb down into a canyon, it's important that you figure out how you're going to get out.

Aron Ralston and the boulder that trapped his arm

4   TALK ABOUT IT

A Work in pairs. Use **Language Bank 27** to help you.
Student A: Close your book. Pretend to be Rex Tanner, talking about Aron Ralston. Give your opinion of what he should/could have done. Start like this:
- There are a lot of things he should have done.
Student B: With your book open, help Student A by asking questions, for example:
- What's your opinion of the media reports on Ralston's adventure?

B Work in groups. Discuss these questions and then report back to the rest of the class.
1   Why do people set out on adventures? Do they look for danger?
2   Can you think of any other real-life survival stories?

C Answer these questions, yes (**Y**) or no (**N**). Give evidence to support your answers.

	Y / N
1 Does Rex Tanner think that everything Ralston did was wrong?	☐
2 Does he think that Ralston should have done all the things he suggests?	☐
3 Do you think Tanner was pleased that the media turned Ralston into a hero?	☐

Surviving disaster

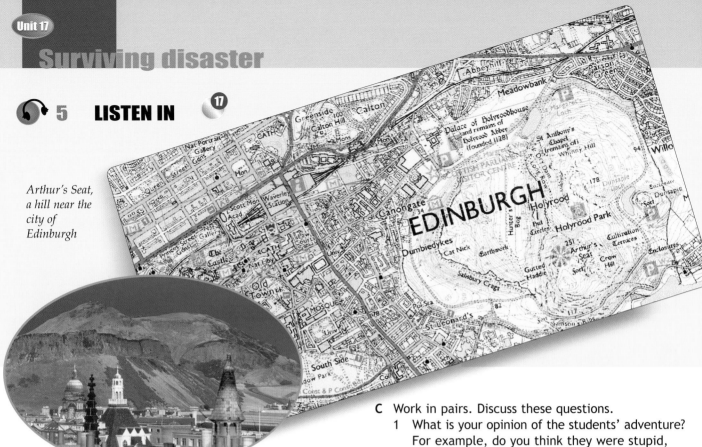

Arthur's Seat, a hill near the city of Edinburgh

🎧 5   LISTEN IN   ⑰

A Before you listen, read these expressions and predict what happened.
* sunny April day
* T-shirt and jeans
* it started snowing
* she slipped
* I thought I was going to pass out
* I had brought a mobile phone
* it hovered directly above us
* when I woke up, I was in hospital

B Listen to three Edinburgh University students talking about something they did and then complete the sentences.

1 Rory thought he should have ... the others about things they needed to do before the climb.
2 Rory is an ... hiker and was wearing the right clothing.
3 Michael thinks that he is quite ... and that the climb was going to be easy.
4 Rory, on the other hand, was ... by how unfit Michael was.
5 Alison ... that it was a bit cold.
6 Michael wanted to go down but Alison ... him to continue.
7 When Alison fell, they ... behind a boulder.
8 Rory offered Alison his pullover because she was ....
9 Alison was ... with herself for being so stupid.
10 Michael remembers the helicopter, which ... above them.

C Work in pairs. Discuss these questions.
1 What is your opinion of the students' adventure? For example, do you think they were stupid, brave or both? Give reasons for your opinion.
2 What do you think would have happened if Michael had gone down earlier?
3 Do you ever go hill walking? Explain what you should do when hiking.

6   CONTROVERSY

Student A is a sailor who has been rescued by Student B, who is captain of the lifeboat. Student C is a journalist trying to find out what happened.

  SEE ROLE CARDS FOR UNIT 17

7   PORTFOLIO WRITING

Write a story (170 - 200 words) about a survival experience in the wilderness, or at sea. Choose a story you know or invent one. Use the following guidelines.

Title:	*Lucky to survive.*
Set the scene:	*Describe the place, the weather and the people you were with.*
Explain your plan:	*We planned to set out early ...*
What you did:	*We set off at midday ...*
What you should have done:	*We should have made sure we had mobile phones with us, but ...*
What happened:	*John was walking along the path ...*
Useful words:	*fall, injure, break, call for help, danger, ambulance*
Conclusion:	*We learnt some important lessons about ... We shouldn't have ... We could have ...*

8 PHYSICAL GEOGRAPHY in English

People who live on Lake Titicaca can survive the thin air at high altitudes

SUPERMEN OF THE ANDES

Lake Titicaca is 3,821 metres (12,530 feet) above sea level, in the Andes mountains of Peru and Bolivia. Visitors to the lake often suffer from altitude sickness. This was discovered in the 1920s by a Peruvian doctor, Carlos Monge. "A victim of severe altitude sickness is short of breath and light-headed, has headaches and a rapid heartbeat. But Andean man is a kind of superman," Dr Monge wrote, describing how local people live normally at high altitudes with much less oxygen in the air.

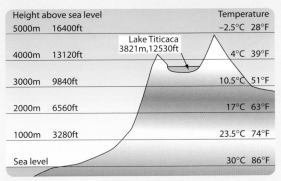

Height above sea level		Temperature	
5000m	16400ft	−2.5°C	28°F
4000m	13120ft	4°C	39°F
3000m	9840ft	10.5°C	51°F
2000m	6560ft	17°C	63°F
1000m	3280ft	23.5°C	74°F
Sea level		30°C	86°F

Lake Titicaca 3821m, 12530ft

The temperature drops by 1°C for every 150m of altitude

Today, doctors know more about how people adapt to the thin air. "Andeans solve the problem by having more haemoglobin in their blood," says Dr Rosie Brewer, a research scientist. "Haemoglobin carries oxygen through the blood. Having more haemoglobin reduces the effects of altitude sickness."

The people of the Andes have also adapted to other dangers of living at high altitudes. Up there the sun is much stronger, even though the air is colder. There is less than half the dust and water in the air at 2,500m (8,000 feet), compared to sea level. This means that more of the sun's ultraviolet rays can get through and cause severe sunburn.

A Read the text and answer the questions:
1 If the temperature is 10°C at sea level, what is the temperature at 1,500m above sea level?
2 What is altitude sickness? Do airline passengers suffer from it?
3 What does haemoglobin do?
   (a) carry oxygen?   (b) reduce altitude sickness?
4 What kind of rays cause sunburn?

B Give advice to some people from sea level, who are going hiking near Lake Titicaca. Advise them on: how to plan; what they should take with them; what to wear; what dangers to expect; how to get help.

9 INTERACTIVE TASK

Work in pairs. Hold a four-minute conversation.
Student A: Choose a sentence as a conversation starter. Choose one that you can continue speaking about.
● I think the wilderness should be left to the wild animals.
● I read a story about people who were caught in a storm.
● A friend of mine thinks people who have an accident should pay for the cost of their rescue. I'm not so sure.

Student B: Take control of the conversation by asking for more information and giving your opinion. Here are some suggestions:
● In other words, it was really dangerous?
● Tell me more.
● Really? Why do you think that?
● What you should have done is …

10 *Your answer:* ARE YOU A SURVIVOR?

Having read this unit, what do you think? Discuss these questions with the rest of the class. Here are some suggestions to help you with the answers.
A Could you have survived in Ralston's situation?
● No. I don't think I could have cut off my arm.
● But I think I would have been more careful. I'd have told someone about my trip.
B Are you a survivor?
● Yes, I think I could keep my head in a dangerous situation.
● I'm not sure. I give up quite easily.
C What's the most adventurous thing you've ever done?
● I've never done anything adventurous! I like a quiet life!
● I've been rock-climbing. That was very exciting.

Alone in space?

What's new?

Subject:	The supernatural
Function:	Hypothesising
Grammar:	*must / might / could / can't* + present perfect

1 *The BIG question:* ARE WE ALONE IN SPACE?

FACT: A survey revealed that five million Americans believe they have seen UFOs.

(a)

(b)

(c)

2 PREVIEW

Words:

A Which of the following does photo (a) show? You can give more than one answer.

1 A visual illusion ☐
2 Aliens arriving from outer space ☐
3 A secret military aircraft ☐
4 A UFO (unidentified flying object) ☐

B Which of the following do photos (b) and (c) show?

1 the Sun, a star ☐
2 the universe ☐
3 a comet ☐
4 Saturn, a planet ☐
5 the solar system ☐
6 a galaxy ☐

C Number the items in activity B from smallest to largest.

Language: Read these sentences and then answer the questions.

- People could have invented the stories in order to attract publicity.
- People might have imagined these experiences.
- Spacemen can't have visited the Earth at some time in the past .... can they?
- They must have learnt them by watching the sky.

Which of these sentences:

A refers to the past?
B refers to a past possibility?
C refers to a deduction?
D have more or less the same meaning?
E makes a statement about the past that is almost certainly true?

SEE WORKBOOK UNIT 18

Ideas: The following sentences are from the reading text on the opposite page. Read them and then answer the questions.

- Kenneth Arnold claimed that he saw nine shining disks travelling at about 1,200 miles an hour.
- Most scientists don't believe that our planet has been visited by aliens.
- There was a story that an alien spacecraft must have crashed in the New Mexico desert near Roswell, USA.
- Members of an African tribe believe that they have knowledge given to them by spacemen.

A Which of these statements is the most extraordinary in your opinion? Say why.
B What do you think Kenneth Arnold might have seen?
C What do you think a spaceman might look like?

3 READING

A Read the text quickly and number the sentences (1–7) in the correct order. Suggest a title for the missing paragraph (g).

(a) Strange knowledge of an African tribe ☐

(b) People see dead alien bodies ☐

(c) Psychologists' explanation for UFOs ☐

(d) A man sees UFOs in the sky ☐

(e) Government explanation for 'alien bodies' ☐

(f) Learned from watching the sky ☐

(g) .... ☐

B Read the first two paragraphs and write true (T), false (F) or maybe (M) beside these sentences. **T / F / M**

1 Kenneth Arnold wasn't the only person to see a UFO in 1947. ☐

2 An alien spacecraft crashed in New Mexico. ☐

3 People saw doctors examining the alien bodies. ☐

C Read paragraphs 3 and 4 and complete these sentences.

1 A 1994 government report did not accept that ....

2 Psychologists think that people might have invented UFO experiences because ....

3 If you are suggestible, it is easy for you to ....

D Read the last three paragraphs and answer these questions.

1 What do the Dogon tribe believe?

2 Why is it strange that they know this?

3 Who might have told them about the night sky?

4 TALK ABOUT IT

Use **Language Bank 28** to help you with these answers.

A Do you think that people have seen real UFOs or real aliens?

B How do you explain the Dogon tribe's strange knowledge of astronomy?

C Do you know any UFO stories? If so, describe them and say what you think might have, or must have happened.

MAYBE WE ARE NOT ALONE?

Sirius A, the brightest star in the Milky Way, and its companion Sirius B

One of the 'alien bodies' found after the Roswell Incident

1 Consider this ...
In 1947, an American pilot and businessman, Kenneth Arnold, claimed that he saw nine shining discs travelling at about 1,200 miles an hour, far faster than any aircraft could travel at the time. On that same day, another pilot saw a group of what were called Unidentified Flying Objects. Soon, people from all over the world began seeing UFOs.

2 Or this ...
Also in 1947, there was a story that an alien spacecraft must have crashed in the New Mexico desert near Roswell, USA. People arriving at the scene said they saw dead and injured alien bodies. Later, a film was shown which seemed to show doctors examining the alien bodies.

3 On the other hand ...
A 1994 government report concluded that the alien bodies at Roswell were actually dummies made to resemble humans. They had been sent up in balloons for research and had fallen from the sky.

4 In reality ...
Most scientists don't believe that our planet has been visited by aliens. Psychologists give a number of explanations for these UFO experiences. They suggest that people could have invented them in order to attract publicity. Alternatively, they say it is likely that people might have imagined them. Once a small number of people started reporting these phenomena, other suggestible people could easily imagine similar experiences.

5 But how about this?
Members of an African tribe called the Dogon, who live in the Republic of Mali, believe that they have knowledge given to them by spacemen from the star Sirius. Dogon mythology, which is hundreds of years old, says that Sirius has a dark companion that is not visible in the sky. In fact, Sirius does have a dark companion, known as Sirius B, but this was not discovered until 1862, so the Dogon people couldn't have learnt of this from modern science. They have diagrams that show the spinning of a spacecraft, and say that it sent out a flame when it touched the Earth. A popular book was written about this in 1977.

6 How on earth ...
... could the Dogons have learned these things? They must have learned them by watching the sky. But these things are only visible with a telescope. There must be a rational explanation. Spacemen can't have visited earth at some time in the past ...... can they?

7 Probably not, but ...
Scientists think that the story started in the 1920s when French missionaries and anthropologists visited the Dogon. Maybe they could have told them something about modern astronomy and the people of the tribe could have combined their traditional beliefs with things the French told them.

🎧 5 LISTEN IN

A Before you listen to the interview, read these statements. Write true (**T**), false (**F**) or maybe (**M**) beside each one.

T/F/M

- There are many stars with planets orbiting round them. ☐
- There are other forms of intelligent life in the universe. ☐
- Scientists have discovered water on Mars. ☐
- Radio telescopes have received signals from outer space. ☐
- The universe began with an explosion. ☐
- The Big Bang was created by God. ☐

B Listen to the interview and check if your answers to A are correct.

C Listen again and answer these questions.
1 Does Simon believe that there is intelligent life in space?
2 Does he think that aliens have visited Earth?
3 How does Simon think the Big Bang started?

D Work in groups of four.
1 How many in your group believe that a Higher Intelligence than man created the universe?
2 Think of three arguments in favour of a Higher Intelligence, for example:
- Something must have started the Big Bang. It didn't start by itself.
3 Think of three arguments against a Higher Intelligence, for example:
- There can't be a God. Life is too cruel.
4 Present your arguments to the class. The class chooses the best arguments for and against. Now take a vote:
- Did a Higher Intelligence create the universe?

6 CONTROVERSY

Pair A witnessed the Roswell Incident and believe that aliens must have visited the Earth. Pair B think there's a rational explanation and that aliens don't exist.

SEE ROLE CARDS FOR UNT 18

Mars   *Spacecraft on Mars*

7 PORTFOLIO WRITING

Imagine that you have had a UFO experience. Write an article for a UFO magazine describing what happened (170 - 200 words). Make a plan like this:

Introduction: Explain that this is the story of a UFO experience you have had. Give some information about yourself, and say when and where the incident took place.

Example:
- At the time, my sister and I were staying in a cottage about two kilometres away from the nearest village.

The story: Describe the spaceship, the aliens and what happened. Describe your feelings.

Example:
- I saw a silver disc spinning about 100 metres above the trees. I couldn't believe my eyes!

Conclusion: Explain why you are sure you had a UFO experience.

Example:
- People say that I might have imagined the whole thing, but if so, why did I have burns on my face?

⑧ ASTRONOMY *in English*

The Solar System:

| Mercury | Venus | Earth | Mars | Jupiter | Saturn | Uranus | Neptune | Pluto |

- Travelling at the **speed of light** (299,792,458 metres per second), it would take seven hours to get from Earth to Pluto. In 2006 scientists decided that Pluto was too small to be considered as a **planet**.
- Our nearest neighbour in the **cosmos**, the star Proxima Centauri, is 4.3 **light years** away.
- To reach it by spaceship would take at least 25,000 years.

Is there life in outer space? Our home, the Milky Way Galaxy, which may have up to four hundred billion 5
stars like our Sun, is only one of a hundred and forty billion other galaxies. There could be as many as ten
billion trillion planets. It is therefore a **statistical probability** that there are millions of other life forms
and civilisations in the universe. If **extraterrestrial life** does exist, it is possible that it is based on
elements other than the carbon, hydrogen, oxygen and nitrogen on which we depend. Some scientists think
it is possible that the chemical element **silicon** could be the basis for other forms of life. Silicon life forms 10
might be so different from our own that we might not recognise them if we saw them.

A Read the text and then:
1 Check the meanings of the seven words and phrases in **bold**.
2 Give four examples of the vastness of the cosmos.
3 Explain why it is likely that there is intelligent life elsewhere in the universe.
4 Explain in what way extraterrestrial life might be different from our own.

⑨ YOUR TOPIC

Work in pairs. Choose a topic for a five-minute talk that is related to this unit, for example:
- Do ghosts exist?

Student A:
- Make notes on the main points of your topic.
- Try and use one or two little stories to illustrate your points.
- Prepare to answer any questions that Student B may ask. Practise your talk, using your notes.
- Give your talk to Student B. Listen to Student B's comments, and change your talk, if necessary.
- Give your talk to the whole class.

Student B:
- Note down questions that you want to ask.
- Listen to Student A's talk carefully and ask questions. Answer any questions he/she asks. Also ask for clarification, if there is something you don't understand (See **Language Bank 5**).

⑩ *Your answer:* ARE WE ALONE IN SPACE?

Having read this unit, what do you think? Discuss these questions with the rest of the class. Here are some suggestions to help you with the answers.

A Have aliens ever visited earth?
- Possibly. Many people claim that they've seen UFOs.
- In my opinion, they must have imagined it.
B Are we alone in space?
- The universe is so vast that it's likely there are other forms of intelligent life.
- Perhaps we are alone. We haven't found any radio signals from outer space yet.
C What kind of life forms might there be?
- They might not be life forms we would recognise.

1 *The BIG read*: *WEST WITH THE NIGHT* by Beryl Markham

Beryl Markham was an Englishwoman who lived much of her life in Africa. At the age of 18, she became a race-horse trainer, and later she became an airline pilot. In 1936, she was the first person to fly solo across the Atlantic from Europe. She took off from England and landed in Canada, 21 hours later. In her autobiography, she describes her arrival in Nova Scotia in her plane, *The Gull*.

2 PREVIEW

A Before you read, decide if these statements are true (T) or false (F). **T / F**

1 A plane needs a tank that contains petrol in order to fly. ☐

2 A plane can take off and land at the same time. ☐

3 A plane has an engine, propeller and wheels. ☐

B Read the introduction above and answer the questions.

1 In what ways was Beryl Markham unusual?

2 Where did *The Gull* land?

C Read the text quickly for gist. Match the words in **bold** in the text with these definitions.

1	how high something is	6	ground that is always very wet
2	very soft, wet earth	7	shake
3	a small simple building	8	when you don't succeed
4	ground	9	stops
5	land that is covered by water	10	belief that you are able to do things well

3 READING

A Read Part 1 carefully. Are these sentences true (T) or false (F)? **T / F**

1 At first, Markham believed that her plane wouldn't have any problems. ☐

2 When the engine started shuddering, she thought the problem was an airlock. ☐

3 Markham looked at her map when she was over Cape Breton. ☐

4 When the plane crashed, Markham fell out. ☐

B Find these phrases and answer the questions.

● But who has the right to confidence except the Gods?

● ... the realisation of failure seeped into my heart.

● ... a forced landing was failure ...

● ... even at my present crippled speed ...

1 Why do the Gods have the right to confidence?

2 Did the realisation come quickly or slowly?

3 When does a plane make a forced landing?

4 In what way was the plane crippled?

C Read Part 2. Choose the correct answer.

1 When Markham climbed out of the plane, the first thing she did was: (a) cry (b) look at her watch (c) look for help

2 Markham was found by: (a) a fisherman (b) a citizen of Hades (c) a crowd of people

3 The Cape Breton islander took Markham to: (a) Sydney Airport (b) a telephone (c) Floyd Bennett Field

4 For a while Markham felt ...... about her flight. (a) disappointed (b) pleased (c) excited

4 TALK ABOUT IT

A What do we learn from this extract about Beryl Markham's attitude to success and failure?

B Judging from this extract, is Markham an optimist or a pessimist? Give reasons for your opinion.

C What are your feelings towards Markham on reading this extract? Do you admire her bravery?

5 PORTFOLIO WRITING

Write a newspaper report about Markham's solo flight across the Atlantic (170 - 200 words).

21

1 Success breeds **confidence**. But who has the right to confidence except the Gods? I had a following wind, my last tank of petrol was more than three-quarters full, and the world was as bright to me as if it were a new world, never touched. If I had been wiser, I might have known that such moments are, like innocence, short-lived. My engine began to **shudder** before I saw the **land**. It died, it spluttered, it started again and limped along. 5

There are words for everything. There was a word for this – airlock, I thought. This had to be an airlock because there was petrol enough. I thought I might clear it by turning on and turning off all the empty tanks, and so I did that, but the effort wasn't any good, and I lost **altitude** slowly while the realisation of failure seeped into my heart. If I made the land, I should have been the first to fly the North Atlantic from England, but from my point of view, from a pilot's point of view, a forced landing was **failure** because New York was my goal. If only I could land and then take off, I would make it still … if only, if only … 10 15

I find the land. Visibility is perfect now and I see land forty or fifty miles ahead. If I am on my course, that will be Cape Breton. Minute after minute goes by. The land is under me. I snatch my map and stare at it. I am, even at my present crippled speed, only twelve minutes from Sydney Airport, where I can land for repairs and then go on. 20 25

The engine **cuts** once more and I begin to glide, but now I am not worried; she will start again, as she has done, and I will gain altitude and fly into Sydney.

But she doesn't start. This time she's dead as death; *The Gull* settles earthward and it isn't any earth I know. It is black earth stuck with boulders and I hang above it, on hope and on a motionless propeller. Only I cannot hang above it long. The earth hurries to meet me, my wheels touch, and I feel them submerge. I go forward, striking my head on the glass of the cabin front, hearing it shatter, feeling blood pour over my face. 30 35

2 I stumble out of the plane and sink to my knees in muck and stand there foolishly staring, not at the lifeless land, but at my watch.

Twenty-one hours and twenty-five minutes.

Atlantic flight. Abingdon. England, to a nameless **swamp** – non-stop. 40

A Cape Breton islander found me – a fisherman trudging over the **bog** saw me floundering in the embracing soil of his native land. I had been wandering for an hour and the black mud had got up to my waist and the blood from the cut in my head had met the **mud** halfway. 45

From a distance, the fisherman directed me with his arms and with shouts toward the firm places in the bog, and for another hour I walked on them and came towards him like a citizen of Hades* blinded by the sun, but it wasn't the sun; I hadn't slept for forty hours. 50

He took me to his **hut** on the edge of the coast and I found that built upon the rocks there was a little cubicle that housed an ancient telephone – put there in case of shipwrecks. 55

I telephoned to Sydney Airport to say that I was safe. On the following morning I did step out of a plane at Floyd Bennett Field and there was a crowd of people waiting to greet me, but the plane I stepped from was not *The Gull*, and for days while I was in New York I kept thinking about that and wishing over and over again that it had been *The Gull*, until the wish lost its significance, and time moved on. 60

*In Greek mythology, Hades was a place under the earth where the dead continued to exist.

Extract from *West with the Night,* by Beryl Markham, published by Virago Modern Classics, reproduced by permission of Pollinger Ltd.

Key:
Student's Book Page *18*
Workbook Unit *Wu6*
Listening Unit *Au12*

Unit 0
Think global, act local
See pages 4-7

advantage	a benefit; something that is good	4
agricultural	relating to farming	4
aim	why you are doing something; what you want to happen as a result of what you are doing	*Wu 0*
based	if something such as a company is based somewhere, that is where its offices are	*Wu 0*
beef	the meat that comes from cows and bulls	4
briefly	using not very many words	6
cattle	cows and bulls	7
chef	a person who cooks in a restaurant	5
citrus fruit	fruit such as oranges, lemons and grapefruit	*Wu 0*
coal	a hard black substance that comes from the ground and that is burnt for fuel	6
combine, to	to join one thing with another	7
controversy	a lot of serious discussion, involving strong feelings	6
cut down, to	to reduce; to make smaller	7
dairy produce	milk, cheese, butter etc.	4
developed country	a wealthy industrial country	7
developing country	a poor country that doesn't have much industry	7
disadvantage	the opposite of a benefit	4
distance	how far it is between two places	4
economics	the study of the way money, business and industry work	7
economy	the money that comes from business and industry	7
exhibition	a show of things to look at, for example in a museum	6
face competition, to	if a company faces competition, another company is doing the same thing	*Wu 0*
farmers' market	a market that sells food from local farms	4
gap	a space	5
gas	the gas fuel you use for cooking and heating (UK); petrol, the liquid fuel used in cars (US)	7
greengrocer	a person who runs a shop that sells fruit and vegetables	*Wu 0*
grow, to	to get bigger	7
honey	the sweet substance made by bees	5
hypermarket	a very large supermarket	4
independent	an independent shop is one that is not part of a group or chain	4
iPod	a small electronic device for listening to music	5
item	a thing	4
laptop computer	a small computer	4
local	relating to the area where you live	4
location	where a person or thing is	*Wu 0*
mango	a tropical fruit	4
manufactured	made in a factory	4
materials	substances such as paper, stone and plastic, from which things are made	6
million	1,000,000 (UK), 1.000.000	*Au 0*
minerals	metals and other substances found in the ground	4
move, to	if you move to an area, you go and live there	5
mug	a kind of large cup	5
neighbourhood	the area where you live	4

oil	the black substance that petrol (UK) and gas (US) are made from	*Au 0*
plate	what you eat your food off	5
pottery	hand-made cups, plates etc.	5
precious	valuable	*Au 0*
rapidly	very fast	7
recycle, to	to re-use; to process something so that it can be used again	6
regional	relating to a particular area	5
shopkeeper	a person who owns and runs a small shop	*Wu 0*
souvenir	something that you buy when you are on holiday to take home with you	4
successful	which is doing well	*Wu 0*
take-away food	food that you buy at a shop to eat immediately or at home	5
textiles	different kinds of cloth	4
theme park	a large area where people go for entertainment	6
throw away, to	to get rid of something, because you don't want it	*Au 0*
timber	wood	4
trash (US)	rubbish	6
tuna	a kind of large fish	4
tyre (UK), tire (US)	the black, rubber part of a car wheel	6
vase	what you fill with water and put flowers in	5
washing powder	the dry substance you use to wash your clothes with	4
waste	rubbish; what is left over and not wanted	6
wheat	the cereal used to make flour for bread and pasta etc.	4

Unit 1
Mr and Ms Right
See pages 8-11

amusing	funny	9
arranged marriage	a marriage decided by your parents, for example for religious reasons	10
astonishing	very surprising	11
careful be, to	to take care not to put yourself in a dangerous situation	11
confederate	a person who is working with someone else	11
conform, to	to behave in the way you are expected to, or like other members of a group	11
conformity	behaving in the way people expect you to, or like others	11
considerate	a considerate person pays attention to other people's needs	10
crazy for ...	mad about ...	9
crowded	very busy	8
darling	an affectionate way of addressing someone	*Au1*
date	an appointment to go out with someone; the person you go out with	8
desire to conform	a wish not to be different from other people	11
fair	just; right	10
fit	strong and healthy	10
friendship	the relationship that exists between friends	8
gay	homosexual	*Au1*
go ahead, to	to proceed; to continue	*Au1*
go out with someone, to	to date someone, to see them as a girlfriend or boyfriend	10
good-looking	attractive	10
hardworking	if you are hardworking, you work very hard	10

health-food store	a shop that sells natural foods, and vitamins etc.	9
hold	if you have a hold on something, you are in control of it or understand it	9
identity	who you are	9
lonely	unhappy and alone	Wu1
majority, the	most people	11
mate	a partner	9
miserable	very unhappy	Au1
Mr Right	the right man for you as a partner	8
Ms	a title used by women instead of either Miss or Mrs	8
night out	a night spent on a date, for example at a club or restaurant	9
nightlife	entertainment such as clubs and theatres that you go to at night	9
on air	live on radio	Au1
partner	a girlfriend or boyfriend, or the person you live with	9
passionate	having very strong feelings	9
personal ads	small advertisements made by people looking for a girlfriend or boyfriend	8
phone-in	a radio programme that people can phone	Au1
psychologist	a person who studies how people's minds work	11
psychology	the study of how people's minds work	11
relationship	the way in which two or more people are connected	8
romance	the relationship between two people who are in love	8
romantic	a romantic person does things that make their partner feel special	9
sense of humour	if you have a sense of humour, you can see the funny side of things	10
sensitive	understanding and aware of other people's needs	10
single	not married	10
slim	not fat	Au1
sociable	friendly	Au1
subject	a person taking part in a test	11
suburbs	the areas away from the centre of a city	9
superhero	a really exceptional man	Au1
surf, to	to look at a website; to look for something on the internet	9
take something up, to	to start practising something	10
trial	a test	11
word is getting around, the	people are beginning to know	9

Unit 2
Bright lights, big city
See pages 12-15

accommodation	where you live or stay	13
be ruined, to	to be spoilt; to be badly damaged	12
blackout	a situation in which there is no electricity and so no lights	13
bohemian	an unconventional, artistic person	13
camp	an area with lots of tents where people live	Wu2
cappuccino	a kind of milky coffee	12
chart	a table of information	15
clam	a kind of shellfish (creatures from the sea but not fish)	13
congestion	a lot of traffic in the same place	15
corn	cereal crops (wheat, barley etc.); maize	12

crab	a sea creature that has 10 legs and that you can eat	13
derived from	which comes from	12
developed world, the	wealthy industrial countries	15
developing world, the	poor countries with little industry	15
economic migrant	a person who goes from one place to another for work	14
emigration	the movement of people out of a place to somewhere else	14
ethnic minority	a relatively small racial group	14
exhausted	very tired	13
exotic	unusual, interesting and foreign	12
Gay Pride parade	a procession of gay people who are proclaiming their rights	12
groan	an unhappy noise, or one made because you have a pain	13
hectic	very busy	12
high-rise buildings	tall buildings, often with flats	Wu2
human geography	the study of human population	15
immigration	the movement of people into a place from somewhere else	14
in the heart of	in the middle of	13
inner city	in or near the city centre, where there are often social problems	15
interviewee	a person who is being interviewed	14
lobster	a sea creature that has two long claws and that you can eat	13
location	where something is	15
manhole	a large hole in the road that is covered by a piece of metal	13
Midwest, the	the north and central region of the United States	13
migration	the movement of people from one area to another	14
overcrowding	too many people living in too small an area	15
parking lot (US)	a car park	13
peaceful	quiet, calm	12
political refugee	a person who has left their own country because of political problems	14
poverty	a serious lack of money	15
power cut	a period of time when the electricity supply is stopped	12
real money	large amounts of money	13
remote	isolated	12
rural areas	country areas	15
shortage	a lack	15
sidewalk (US)	a pavement	12
sip, to	to drink a little at a time	12
skyscraper	a very tall building, generally with offices	Wu2
spill, to	if you spill a liquid, it pours out of its container	14
standard of living	how comfortable your life is in financial and material terms	Wu2
suburban	relating to the areas on the edges of a town or city	12
subway (US)	an underground railway	13
track	the metal lines that trains run on	13
unemployment	a lack of jobs	15
urban area	a town or city	15
wealthy	rich	Wu2
Welsh	from Wales	13

Glossary

Unit 3 — Fame and fortune
See pages 16-19

album	a disc with a lot of songs on it	18
arrogant	proud and unpleasant towards other people	18
audience	the people who are listening to something	18
autograph	the signature of a famous person	16
be deported, to	to be sent out of a country	Wu3
be in the limelight, to	to get a lot of public attention	17
beware of ...	be careful of ... (because you think it is dangerous)	17
burglary	forcing your way into a building and stealing things	16
caption	words printed underneath a picture to explain it	19
charts, the	the list of the most successful pop records	18
co-star, to	to star with someone else	17
Democratic Party	one of the two largest political parties in the US; it is more left-wing than the Republican Party	19
disguise	something that you wear to hide who you really are	17
divorce, to	to stop being married legally	17
drummer	a musician who plays the drums	18
dustbin (UK), trash can (US)	a container for rubbish	17
Eurovision Song Contest	a song competition that takes place every year between European countries	Wu3
fortune	a lot of money; luck	16
gig	a pop concert	18
have ambitions, to	if you have ambitions to do something, you want to do it very much	Au3
Hello! Magazine	a popular magazine that prints stories about celebrities	16
high life, the	an expensive lifestyle involving a lot of parties	17
hit record	a very successful record	Wu3
influence, to	to have an effect on	17
keep oneself to oneself, to	to be private	Wu3
keep up appearances, to	to behave in the way that people expect you to	17
Nobel Prize	a prize awarded every year to people who have done exceptional work	17
occupation	the presence of a foreign army in a country	19
point of view	an opinion	19
privacy	a situation in which other people do not know about what you are doing	16
public recognition	acknowledgement by people in general of the value of something	17
public relations (PR)	the part of an organisation whose job is to get public approval for the organisation	19
publicity interview	an interview designed to get attention for the person being interviewed	18
rob, to	to take money or property	16
robbery	stealing money or property	16
rumour	a story that may not be true	Wu3
say goodbye to something, to	to accept that you can no longer have something	16
single	a record of an individual song	18
speed-dial	a fast or automatic dialling function	17
stalk, to	to follow and annoy or upset someone, especially a famous person	16
stalker	a person who follows and annoys or upsets someone	16
talented	having an ability to do something	16
trappings	everything extra that goes with a particular lifestyle	17
trash can (US), dustbin (UK)	a container for rubbish	17
uncertainty	not being sure about something	16
vacation home (US)	a house used for holidays	17
villa	a large house that stands by itself in a garden	17
work out, to	if something doesn't work out, it doesn't succeed	17
worthwhile	useful and worth the effort	17

Unit 4 — Animal passions
See pages 20-23

Alzheimer's disease	a condition affecting old people in particular, in which the brain stops working properly	Au4
amorous	behaving in a sexual manner	21
animal rights activist	a person who campaigns against the exploitation of animals	22
ape	apes are animals that include chimpanzees, gorillas and humans	23
baboon	a kind of large African monkey	20
be in competition, to	to want the same food etc.	23
bush meat	meat that comes from wild animals	23
chimpanzee	a kind of ape, closely related to humans	20
companion	a friend	21
cosmetics	make-up	Au4
creature	an animal	21
deforestation	the destruction of forests	23
disappear from sight, to	to go so far away that you can't see it any more	21
dive, to	to go beneath the surface of the water	21
dolphin	a kind of mammal that lives in the sea	20
ecology	the study of the relationships between animals, plants, people and the environment	23
ecosystem	all the plants and animals in a place and how they relate to each other	23
embrace	if two creatures are in an embrace, they hold each other	21
endangered	in danger of disappearing completely	22
environmental concerns	worries about the environment	20
extinction	the total disappearance from the world of a creature	22
flipper	the 'arm' of a whale, seal or other sea mammal	20
gibbon	a kind of ape from southern Asia	20
gorilla	a very large, black, African ape	20
grief	the deep sadness you feel when someone dies	20
habitat	the natural environment in which a particular plant or animal lives	23
hunter	a person who chases and kills animals for food or sport	21
inlet	a long, narrow bit of seawater almost surrounded by land	21
joy	great happiness	20
killer whale	a type of black and white whale	20
mammals	animals that generally give birth to babies which drink milk from their mothers	Au4

mate, to	to join sexually	20
mosquito	a small insect that bites and can give people malaria	Au4
National Park	a large area of land where the plants and animals are protected	23
neuroscientist	a scientist who specialises in the nervous system	21
orang-utan	a kind of ape from Asia with orange-brown hair	20
parrot	a kind of bright-coloured, exotic bird	21
pleasure	a feeling of happiness or satisfaction	20
primates	monkeys, apes and humans	22
pup	a young animal	20
purr, to	to make a noise like a happy cat	21
rainforest	thick, tropical forest where it rains a lot	23
relation	a relative	22
resemble, to	to look like	22
resources	things such as food and land that are needed	23
revive, to	to bring back to life	20
sea lion	a type of large animal that lives by and in the sea	20
shark	a type of very large and sometimes dangerous fish	Wu4
sophisticated	complex and intelligent	22
species	an individual type of animal or plant	Au4
starve to death, to	to die because of a lack of food	20
strategy	a technique	21
stroke, to	to touch gently with a long movement	20
survival	continued existence	23
threatened	in danger	23
trap, to	to catch	21
trunk	the long nose of an elephant	21
vivisection	using live animals for scientific experiments	22
whale	the largest type of sea mammal	20

Unit 5   **Did it really happen?**
See pages 24-27

abolish, to	to bring something to an end	27
Abraham Lincoln	President of the United States, 1861–1865, who abolished slavery	27
American Civil War (1861–1865)	a war in America concerning the abolition of slavery	27
be separated, to	to be divided; to be in different places	25
beat, to	to hit	25
bowl	a round dish	24
brandy	a kind of strong alcohol	27
carefree	happy and not having any worries	25
chained	attached using metal links	27
chauffeur	a person who drives other people to places in a car	26
chief	the leader of a tribe or village	27
debt	money that you owe	25
deck	a floor or level on a ship	27
domestic service	work as a servant in someone's house	26
dozen	twelve	25
eventually	after a long time	25
extract	part of a book, printed separately	25
from a distance	from a long way away	25
housemaid	a girl or woman who does housework for other people	26
lord	a man with very high social status	26

mistress	a woman for whom you work	25
oyster	a kind of shellfish (a creature from the sea but not a fish)	25
passage	a corridor	Au5
recall, to	to remember	24
recollection	a memory	24
remind, to	to make you remember something	24
reminder	something that makes you remember something	24
servant	a person who works for someone else in their home	26
stately home	a very large, old house in the country	26
stick	a long thin piece of wood	25
wander, to	to go from one place to another without any real plan	24
whip, to	to hit with a long piece of leather or rope	25

Unit 6   **You are being watched**
See pages 28-31

analogue signal	a kind of signal (not digital)	31
car mechanic	a person who mends cars	29
CCTV	closed-circuit television; a system of cameras used to watch what people are doing	28
constant	happening all the time; not changing	30
curve (of the Earth)	a rounded shape	31
detect, to	to discover	29
display	information on a screen	29
drown, to	to die by breathing in water	28
fingerprint	the unique pattern of lines on your fingers	29
hooligan	hooligans are people who are violent and noisy in public places, for example at football matches	Wu6
horrified	shocked	28
infringement	a lack of respect (for rights, freedom, the law)	Wu6
installed with	fitted with	29
invasion of privacy	something which does not respect your privacy	28
ionosphere	part of the Earth's outer atmosphere	31
liberty	freedom	31
lifeguard	a person at a swimming pool who helps people who are in difficulties	28
manufacturer	the maker of something	30
microchip	a very small electronic device that stores information	30
monitor, to	to watch closely	29
overhead	above you	29
reassured	made to feel less worried	28
RFID tag	a very small 'intelligent' electronic device attached to things so that you know where they are	30
satellite	a device in space often used in communications systems	31
scanner	a device that records and examines images	Wu6
security officer	a person who is responsible for checking who enters and leaves a building	28
smart tag	a very small 'intelligent' electronic device attached to things so that you know where they are	30
splash, to	to hit the water in a noisy way	29
surveillance camera	a camera used to watch people	28
track, to	to follow the movements of something	29

transmit, to	to send out	31
trigger, to	to set something off, such as an alarm	30
unconscious	not aware of what is going on, because of an injury or illness	29
unique	different from anything or anyone else	30
warning signal	a sound or light that tells you that there is a problem	29
wavelength	the size of a radio wave or other type of wave	31

Unit 7 — Oil crisis
See pages 32-35

acid rain	rain that is polluted with gases	35
age	a long period of time (for example the Stone Age)	32
air conditioning	a system that cools the air in a building	34
alternative energy	energy from natural sources, such as solar power or wind power	32
applied science	science used in practical ways	33
atom	the smallest amount of an element	35
barrel	a unit of measurement for oil	33
be used up, to	if something is used up, there is none left	33
bio-fuel	a fuel made from a plant source	33
camel	an animal that lives in the desert and has a hump	32
carbon	an element (C)	35
coal	a hard black substance that comes from the ground and that is burnt for fuel	32
crude oil	oil before it has been refined or purified	35
diesel oil	oil that lorries run on	35
dioxin	a very poisonous substance	35
dramatically	very greatly	32
eco-house	a house that uses technology which respects the environment	34
element	a basic natural substance such as carbon or oxygen which has one type of atom only	35
engineering	design and construction of machines, bridges etc.	33
ethanol	alcohol	33
for lack of ...	because there wasn't enough ...	33
fossil fuel	a fuel such as gas or coal which comes from decayed plants	32
fraction	a part or proportion of something	35
gasoline	petrol	35
greenhouse gases	gases that cause global warming	35
hydrocarbons	a compound that has carbon and hydrogen atoms	35
hydrogen	a gas (H)	32
limitless	infinite	33
Marshal Foch (1851–1929)	the commander of all the Allied armies (Britain, France etc.) during the First World War	33
microscopic	very, very small	35
molecular formula	an abbreviation showing the structure of a chemical substance	35
natural gas	gas for fuel that comes from underground or under the sea	32
oil	the thick black substance from which petrol is made	32
oil crisis	a period in which there is not enough oil	33
oil refinery	an industrial site where oil is purified to make gas and petrol	35

oil rig	a structure in the sea where there is an oil well	35
oil well	a deep hole made in the ground to get oil	32
peak, to	to reach its greatest amount	33
pipe	a long tube that carries a liquid or gas	34
planet	(here) Earth	33
polymer	a kind of chemical compound which has large atoms which are themselves made of smaller atoms of the same type	35
PVC	polyvinyl chloride; a type of plastic	35
renewable energy	energy that will not run out, such as wind power	32
run on, to	to use	34
run out of, to	if you run out of something, you have none of it left	32
solar panel	a square device placed on a roof to catch the energy from the sun	34
solar power	energy from the sun	33
source	where something comes from	33
Stone Age, the	an early period of human history when people used stone tools	33
stove	a cooker	34
supplies	the amount of something that is available for use	32
tank	a large container	34
urgently	very soon	34
vapour	tiny drops of liquid forming a mist	33

Extended reading 1
See pages 36-37

animal run	a path made and used by animals	37
be wounded, to	to have an injury; to be hurt	37
become absorbed, to	to get very interested in something and concentrate on it	37
blurt out, to	to say something very suddenly	37
briar	a wild rose plant with thorns	36
Che succede?	an Italian phrase: What's the matter?	37
consternation	worry and fear	37
contorted	twisted	36
crawl, to	to move on your hands and knees	36
dingy	dull	37
enclosed	in a secret place	37
fathom, to	to understand	37
filthy	very dirty	37
furrow, to	to become lined	37
futilely	without having any effect	37
indignantly	in an annoyed way, because you think something is unfair	37
infinitely	totally	37
invading	an invading army is one that goes into a country by force, as an enemy	37
irritated	annoyed	37
jerk, to	to move suddenly	37
legions of ...	lots and lots of ...	37
lousy	horrible	36
mandolin	a type of musical instrument that has strings	36
paralysed	unable to move	36
pitifully	weakly; in a way that makes you feel sorry for them	37
posture	the position of the body	37
reflect, to	to think	37
reproach, to	to tell someone that they shouldn't have done something	37
ricked	twisted	37
rosemary	a herb used in cooking	37
scrape, to	to scratch	37
shrapnel	bits of metal that come from a bomb when it explodes	36

sigh, to	to let out a long breath	37
snail	a small creature that has a shell on its back	36
sniff, to	to smell	37
strand	a strand of hair is a number of hairs that are together, like a piece of string	36
streak	a long, narrow mark	37
tangle	a mass of things twisted together	36
texture	how something feels (rough, smooth etc.)	37
thorn	a sharp spike on a plant	36
tug, to	to pull	37
tunnel	a passage	36
underside	the side underneath	37
unpatriotic	disloyal to your country; not supportive of your country	37
untangle, to	to take the knots and twists out of something	37
vanish, to	to disappear	37
vulnerable	not safe	36
wound	(past participle of **wind**); twisted	37
yield to temptation, to	to do something that you really want to do after trying not to do it	37

Unit 8 — Exam pressure
See pages 38-41

admission	entry	40
attend, to	to go to	38
commit suicide, to	to kill oneself	39
competition	a situation in which people want the same thing	39
counsellor	a person who gives advice	40
critical thinking	thinking carefully and analytically in order to make a judgement	41
curriculum	the contents of a particular course of study	Wu8
degree	the qualification you get at a university	38
demanding	difficult	Wu8
diploma	a qualification	38
distressed	anxious and upset	39
drop, to	if you drop a subject, you stop studying it	Wu8
enrol, to	to join a university etc. to study there	41
facilities	buildings and services (library, accommodation etc.)	Au8
fears	things that worry you	39
fee	the money you have to pay for some services or education	40
feel homesick, to	to miss your family and your home	40
graduate	a person who has completed a degree	38
helpline	a telephone service that people can call for advice	38
intense	very strong	39
journal	a specialised magazine which contains academic articles	41
last minute	at the latest possible time	Wu8
leaflet	a small book or piece of paper with information	38
peer	your peers are people who are the same age as you	41
private education	education that you have to pay for	39
reform	change and improvement	39
SAT Test	a test that you have to pass in order to go to a college	38
scholarship	money to pay for studying	Wu8
semester	one half of the school year	40

sensible	reasonable; not stupid	Au8
spokesman	a person who represents others and speaks for them	39
talent	a natural ability (for music etc.)	41
tragedy	a very sad event	39
undergraduate	a student who is studying for a first degree	38
union	an organisation that protects the rights of workers	39

Unit 9 — Give peace a chance
See pages 42-45

air force	the armed service that fights in the air	42
aircraft carrier	a large ship that carries aeroplanes	42
armed service	the army, navy or air force	42
arms	guns and bombs	42
assault rifle	a large gun used by soldiers	42
bulldozer	a large machine for moving earth	44
civilian	a person who is not in the armed services	42
Cold War, the	the period after the Second World War when there was tension between the West and Russia	45
combat	fighting	43
concentration camp	a prison where millions of Jews died during the Second World War	Wu9
conflict	a battle; fighting	43
demonstrate, to	to protest	44
foreign minister	the person in a government who is responsible for relations with other countries	45
Gaza Strip, the	an area of land fought over by Palestine and Israel	43
genie out of the bottle	if the genie is out of the bottle, a big and probably bad change has taken place	42
genocide	the murder of a lot of people because of their race	45
helicopter	a kind of aircraft that uses spinning blades and that doesn't have wings	42
immoral	not moral; wrong	44
land mine	a kind of bomb buried in the ground	42
machine gun	a gun which fires a lot of bullets very quickly	42
missile	a kind of bomb that travels through the air	42
mission	a special military task	45
moral	right; just	44
motherland, the	one's own country	43
Muslim	a follower of Islam	45
navy	the armed service that fights at sea	42
on horseback	while riding a horse	Wu9
peace activist	a person who campaigns for peace	44
peacekeeper	a soldier who tries to prevent war and fighting	45
peacetime	a period without war	Wu9
pilot	a person who flies an aeroplane	44
primary	most important	43
Red Army	Russia's Communist army	43
revolutionary	relating to a political revolution (when people use force to change a political system)	43
rifle	a kind of gun	42
sleep soundly, to	to sleep very well and peacefully	43

submachine gun	a kind of fairly small machine gun	43
United Nations, the	an international organisation that works for peace	45
volunteer	a person who does something because they want to and who isn't paid	44

Unit 10
I must have one of those
See pages 46-49

adjust, to	if you adjust to something, you adapt and change	47
bury, to	to cover up	Au10
downshift, to	to move somewhere smaller or cheaper	47
extravagant	a person who is extravagant spends a lot of money on unnecessary things	Wu10
former	a word that describes what used to belong to you	47
foul	disgusting	48
fumes	gases	48
garbage (US)	rubbish	48
hi-fi	a stereo system for listening to records	46
household	all the people who are living together in one house	49
living standards	how comfortable your life is in terms of money and material goods	46
mean	not generous	Wu10
medical waste	rubbish that comes from hospitals etc.	Au10
miss out on, to	not to have or not to take part in something enjoyable	48
mp3 player	a small electronic device that lets you listen to music	46
panoramic view	a view all around	47
penniless	without any money	Wu10
rot, to	to go bad	48
rubbish dump	a large area where rubbish is left	48
scavenge, to	to look for useful things among rubbish	48
shack	a small, badly built hut	48
syringe	a device used to give injections	48
township	a poor urban area	Au10
toxic	poisonous	48
tram	a vehicle used for public transport which runs on tracks and is powered by electricity	48
wristband	a plastic bracelet worn to show that you support a particular cause	Wu10
yacht	a large boat with sails or an engine, used for leisure	46

Unit 11
Globesity
See pages 50-53

arctic	very, very cold	50
be obsessed, to	if you are obsessed with something, you think about it all the time	50
chubby	a little bit fat	Wu11
doughnut	a kind of cake that is fried	50
editor-in-chief	the editor with overall responsibility for a publication	51
equation	a situation in which things are properly balanced	53
faint with hunger	so hungry that you feel as though you are going to lose consciousness	52
fitness club	a centre which you can join and where you do exercise	52
folk	people	50
globesity	an invented word: global (relating to the whole world) + obesity (being very fat)	50
gluttonous	very greedy	Wu11

go on a diet, to	to eat less food or eat differently in order to lose weight	52
greedy	if someone is greedy, they eat more than necessary	Wu11
gymnasium	a place where there are exercise machines to help you keep fit	52
humid	damp	51
imbalance	a lack of balance	53
in a row	in succession; one after the other	51
junk food	fast food that isn't good for your health	50
malnutrition	not having enough food; not having the right kinds of things in your diet	53
natural resources	all the land, minerals, forests and sources of energy	51
obese	very fat	50
overweight	too heavy	50
physical education	exercise classes in schools	Wu11
pick on, to	to criticise unfairly	51
ravenous	very, very hungry	Wu11
shapely	having an attractive body	Wu11
skinny	very thin	Wu11
slender	slim; not fat	Wu11
starving	very, very hungry; dying because of a lack of food	Wu11
sultry	unpleasantly warm and airless	50
weights	objects that you lift to build bigger muscles	52
well-built	fairly big	Wu11
work out, to	to do a programme of exercise	52

Unit 12
Cities of the future
See pages 54-57

accessibility	how easy or not a place is to get to	54
ambitious	big, daring and needing a lot of work	55
anchor	a heavy object dropped from a boat to stop it from moving	56
architecture	the design and study of buildings	57
be madness, to	to be crazy	55
bend, to	to change the shape of something so that it is no longer straight	56
billion	a thousand million (1,000,000,000)	54
cosmopolitan	having an international feel	57
craftspeople	people skilled at making things by hand	57
criteria	things you take into account when making a decision	54
dome	a rounded roof, like half a ball	Wu12
drift, to	to move slowly, following the natural movement of air or water	56
earthquake	a shaking of the ground	55
float, to	to sit on the surface of water; to rest just above something	Wu12
functional	practical	57
futuristic	which looks as though it belongs in the future	55
Great Pyramid of Giza, the	the largest of the Pyramids in Egypt	55 / 54
hollow	with a space right through the middle	56
levitation	lifting from the ground without help	54
link, to	to connect	56
magnet	a piece of metal that attracts other metal objects	Au12
pre-constructed	built in advance	55
ring of fire, the	the chain of volcanoes around the Pacific	56
section	one part of something larger	

seismic	relating to earthquakes	55
storey	a level in a building	55
stretch, to	to extend	55
structure	a building	55
submarine	a kind of boat that travels underwater	Au12
suspended	hanging	55
trendy	fashionable and modern	Wu12
tsunami	a huge wave caused by an underwater earthquake	55
vacuum	an enclosed space without any air in it	56
vertical	that goes upwards, not along the ground	54
volcanic activity	things that volcanoes do (pouring out gas, erupting)	55
volcanic eruption	when a volcano pours out gas, rocks and lava	55
warehouse	a large building where goods are stored	Wu12
withstand, to	to survive; not to be destroyed	55

Unit 13 — Call of the wild
See pages 58-61

amendment	an addition or change to a law	61
barrel	a large, round container	Au13
bear arms, to	to carry guns	61
bullfighter	a person who injures or kills bulls for sport	Wu13
bullring	where bullfights take place	Wu13
call of the wild, the	if you feel the call of the wild, you find wild places very attractive	58
caviar	the eggs from some fish	60
condemn, to	if you condemn something, you think it is morally wrong	61
constitution	the laws of a country and a statement of people's rights	61
copper	a reddish-coloured metal (Cu)	Au13
depend on, to	to need	60
gesture	a movement of the body, such as shaking hands	Wu13
glacier	a large mass of slow-moving ice between mountains	59
guarantee, to	to say that something will definitely happen or be the case	58
harvest, to	(here) to kill	59
hot spring	a stream of hot water that comes out of the ground	59
hunt, to	to chase and kill animals	58
infringe, to	if you infringe a right, you do not respect it	61
justice	fairness to people; the legal system	61
militia	a group of people who act like an army but who are not officially soldiers	61
mine, to	to take something such as coal or metal out of the ground	Au13
mineral deposit	metals and other substances that are found in the ground	60
miss out, to	not to be lucky	58
nickel	a metal (Ni)	60
population density	how many people live in a given area of land	60
posterity	people who will be alive in the future	61
roam, to	to wander	58
salami	a kind of sausage	Au13
salmon roe	the eggs of salmon	60
salted	covered with salt	Au13
soak, to	to cover something with water and leave it	60
stalk, to	to follow a wild animal quietly	59
tranquility	peace (US spelling, UK tranquillity)	61

trophy	something that you keep to show that you have done something of which you are proud	58
untamed	wild	59
welfare	well-being	61
wilderness	an area of wild land	Au13
wrestling match	a kind of fighting competition	60

Extended reading 2 — See pages 62-63

alarmed	very worried	62
cannibalise, to	to take something to pieces which you then use to make something else	62
civic amenity site	a site where you can take materials to be recycled	62
discarded	thrown away	62
dispose of, to	to get rid of; to throw away	63
dump, to	to leave something somewhere because you don't want it	62
Friends of the Earth	an organisation that campaigns on environmental issues	63
grey area	something that isn't entirely clear	62
guidance	advice	62
in working order	not broken	63
injustice	a lack of fairness	62
lead	a metal (Pb)	63
leaded glass	glass that has lead (Pb) in it	62
legislation	laws	63
pose a danger, to	to be potentially dangerous	62
reclassify, to	to change the category of something	63
ship, to	to send by boat	63
sift through, to	to sort through and examine	62
totter	a person who sorts through rubbish for things to sell	62
virus	an illegal program that harms computers	62

Unit 14 — Fantasy worlds
See pages 64-67

be healed, to	to be repaired; to get better	65
beast	a large animal	65
blaze, to	to shine very brightly	65
bound	stopped from moving	65
breach	a space	64
cast a spell, to	to say magic words which will affect what happens	64
cemetery	where dead people are put in the ground	Wu14
clank, to	to make a loud metallic noise	67
confuse, to	to mix things up; to think that one thing is something else	64
daemon	a spirit that looks after you	Wu14
dragon	a mythical animal that breathes fire	64
embrace, to	to hold something close to yourself	65
enchantment	a series of magic words; a spell	64
evil	wicked; very bad	Au14
fabric	material or cloth; the way everything holds together	65
fade, to	to get less bright	65
fairy	a magical creature	64
fled	(past simple of flee); ran away	65
form	a shape	64
genre	a particular type of literature or other art form	67
ghost	the spirit of someone who has died	67
give someone a fright, to	to frighten someone suddenly	Au14

gleam, to	to shine	64
glimmer, to	to shine, but not brightly	65
Gothic novel	a type of supernatural mystery story	67
grave	the hole in the ground in which a person is put after they have died	Wu14
grip, to	to hold something tightly	65
haunt, to	if you say that something unpleasant haunts you, you keep thinking about it	67
hiss, to	to make a sound like -ss-	64
horror movie	a film that is meant to be very frightening	66
horror-stricken	terrified	67
intolerable	unbearable	65
it'll be a relief when ...	I'll be glad when ...	66
lifeless	dead	67
monster	a large, frightening, imaginary creature	67
mystery	something strange which you don't understand	67
outstretched	reaching out	65
oval	a roundish shape, like an elongated circle	64
paw	an animal's foot	65
predecessor	something that comes before something else	64
prophecy	a prediction that something will happen in the future	Wu14
rip	a tear	65
rose	(past simple of **rise**); got up	65
sequel	the next part of a story	66
shiver, to	to shake	65
shrink, to	to get smaller	65
sob, to	to make a noise like crying	65
sorrowful	very sad	65
spark	a small flash	67
speculate, to	to wonder about what something is really like	67
spirit	a supernatural being	65
split apart, to	to break open	65
stagger, to	to walk with difficulty, falling at the same time	65
stir, to	to move a little	67
struggle, to	to move with difficulty	65
supernatural	not belonging to this world	67
suspense	a feeling of fear about what is going to happen	66
terrify, to	to frighten badly	66
terror	a feeling of great fear	66
thriller	a very exciting story	66
tore	(past simple of **tear**); ripped	65
trilogy	a series of three books that make one whole story	65
vampire	a creature that feeds on people's blood	64
vision	something mysterious that you see or believe you have seen	67
whine, to	to make a long, high noise	65
witch	a woman who has magic powers	64
wizard	a man who has magic powers	64
writhe, to	to twist	65

Unit 15   **Think big!**
See pages 68-71

account for, to: financial services account for 1 in 5 jobs	represent a proportion of a total one in five of all jobs are in the financial services sector of industry	71
ambition	something you really want to do	71

apply, to	if you apply for a job, you ask for it formally	70
auto engineering	engineering related to cars	71
be fired, to	to lose your job	Wu15
be hired, to	to get a job	Wu15
be laid off, to	to lose your job, generally because there is not enough work for everyone	Wu15
business services	services for business, such as accounting and management consultancy	71
candidate	a person who has applied for a job	70
civil engineering	engineering for roads, bridges and buildings	Au15
CV	curriculum vitae; a document with details of your education and work experience	Au15
decline	if there is a decline in something, it gets less or smaller	71
entrepreneur	a person who creates businesses and makes business deals	68
experience	an individual thing that happens to you; all the things that happen in your life, your knowledge and skills	68
financial services	services involving money, such as banking and insurance	68
funding	money to pay for something	69
get the sack, to	to lose your job	Wu15
graduate, to	to complete a degree	70
growth	increase	71
human resources	the part of a company that deals with recruiting and training	70
income	the money that a person earns or receives from investments	71
instant success	something that is immediately successful	69
investment bank	a bank that invests its customers' money in other businesses	69
legal services	professional services related to the law, such as buying property or defending someone who believes they have lost their job unfairly	68
manufacturing industry	industry that makes things	71
pharmacist	the person in a chemist's shop who prepares and gives you your medicines	68
promote, to	to give someone a more important job in a company	Wu15
publicity	something which attracts the public's attention	69
racing driver	a person who drives fast cars in races	68
'real-world' experience	experience gained by working and through life generally, not through studying	69
scooter	a small motorbike	Wu15
self-employed	if you are self-employed, you work for yourself	71
service industry	an industry such as banking or transport that provides a service and doesn't produce goods	71
turn down, to	to refuse	69
vet	a person who treats sick animals	68
wage	the money that you are paid every week for work	Wu15

Unit 16   **Throw away the key**
See pages 72-75

amphetamine	a drug that makes people excited	72

atrocity	a dreadful action	75
be convicted, to	to be found guilty of something in a court of law	72
be on parole, to	a person who has been let out of prison early and will stay free as long as they do not commit another crime	74
caffeine	the chemical in coffee that can keep you awake	72
case	a trial; a legal inquiry	Wu16
cell	a small room in a prison where a prisoner stays	74
cocaine	a powerful drug to which you can become addicted	72
come into force, to	to become official	74
court	the place where legal matters are decided by a judge	Wu16
death penalty	the punishment of death	73
Declaration of Human Rights, the	a United Nations document concerning human dignity	75
degrading	humiliating; which doesn't respect people	75
drug addict	a person who takes illegal drugs and cannot stop taking them	73
drug rehabilitation centre	a place where you can go to recover from a problem with drugs	72
drug trafficker	a person who buys and sells illegal drugs	73
ecstasy	an illegal drug that makes people happy and excited	72
gang	a group of people who go around together and cause trouble	73
hard drugs	dangerous drugs that are illegal	72
heroin	a common type of illegal drug to which you can become addicted	72
human rights	the basic rights of everyone (freedom, justice and equality)	75
ice	the popular name for a kind of hard drug	73
irrational	not sensible	73
jail	a prison	73
jeer, to	to shout insults	Wu16
justified	reasonable; acceptable	73
kidnap, to	to take someone away illegally	Au16
last resort	something that is used only if everything else has failed	73
life prisoner	a person who has to spend the rest of their life in prison	74
marijuana	a drug that can be smoked	72
methamphetamine	a kind of hard drug	73
offend, to	to commit a crime	74
overdose	if you take an overdose, you take too much of a drug and die or become very ill	Wu16
policy	an official attitude and way of doing something	73
possession of drugs	having drugs	73
property	things that belong to you	75
prosecutor	a lawyer who tries to prove that someone is guilty	73
psycho-therapist	a person who treats people who are mentally ill, using psychological methods, not medicines	Wu16
put someone away, to	to send someone to prison	74

recreational drugs	drugs that people take with friends, for example when they go clubbing	72
repeat offender	a person who has been convicted of more than one offence	74
sentence	the punishment given by a court of law	74
sentence to death, to	to give someone a punishment of death	73
serve (eight years), to	to spend eight years in prison	Au16
social drugs	illegal drugs that people take with friends	72
soft	not severe in dealing with something	72
soft drugs	less strong, illegal drugs	72
soft punishment	something such as therapy instead of a prison sentence	72
therapy	a form of treatment that doesn't use medicines	72
Three-Strikes Law, the	in California, a law that says that anyone who commits three offences will spend the rest of their life in prison	74
tobacco	the substance in cigarettes	72
tolerate, to	to accept something, even if you don't like it	73
torture	deliberately making someone suffer mentally or physically	75
trafficking	trading (in) drugs	73
triple, to	to multiply by three	72
without distinction of ...	with no difference in attitude towards ...	75

Unit 17 — Surviving disaster
See pages 76–79

against all odds	if you do something against the odds, you succeed although it seemed very unlikely	Wu17
altitude sickness	the unwell feelings you can get high in the mountains	79
amputate, to	to cut off	77
boulder	a very large rock	76
canyon	a very deep river valley with steep, rocky sides	76
cliff	a very high wall of rock, for example at the coast	Wu17
climb, to	to go up rocky mountains etc. using ropes	76
frame of mind	a general feeling and attitude	76
haemoglobin	the chemical in the blood that carries oxygen	79
heartbeat	the rhythm of your heart	79
hike	a long walk in the country	76
hiker	a person who enjoys going for walks in the country	76
hover, to	to stay at the same point in the air	78
keep your head, to	to stay calm	76
lifeboat	a boat that rescues people at sea	78
light-headed	dizzy; feeling as though you might faint	79
lose your head, to	to panic	Wu17
mountaineer	a person who climbs mountains	76
pass out, to	to lose consciousness, to faint	78
pocket knife	a small, folding knife; a penknife	77
presence of mind	if you have presence of mind, you are calm in a difficult situation	Wu17
rock-climbing	climbing in rocky places, using ropes	79
search and rescue	looking for and helping people who are lost or injured	77

search party	a group of people who go to look for anyone who is lost	77
shelter, to	to stay out of the sun and rain, or away from danger	Au17
short of breath	if you are short of breath, you find it difficult to breathe properly	79
slip, to	to fall	78
thin air	air that doesn't contain much oxygen	79
treacherous	very dangerous	Wu17
ultra violet rays	the dangerous rays from the sun that burn	79
unfit	not very strong and healthy	Au17
veteran	a person who has a lot of experience in a particular thing	77

Unit 18   **Alone in space**
See pages 80-83

abduct, to	to take someone away illegally; to kidnap	Wu18
alien	a being from space	80
anthropologist	a person who studies people and societies	81
astronomy	the study of the stars	81
Big Bang, the	the huge explosion that created the universe	82
blinking	coming on and going off	Wu18
comet	a bright object in the night sky which has a long tail	80
cosmos	the whole of space	83
crop circle	an unexplained circle in the middle of a field where cereals are growing	Wu18
extraterrestrial	from somewhere in space	83
flash, to	to come on and go off	Wu18
galaxy	a very large group of stars and planets	80
glow	a faint light	Wu18
gravity	the force which makes things fall to the ground	Au18
Higher Intelligence	a force or being that is more intelligent than man	82
hollow	an area that is lower than the land around it	Wu18
hysteria	panic	Wu18
light year	the distance that light travels in one year	83
microbe	a very tiny living thing	Au18
missionary	a Christian who goes to foreign countries to teach people about Christianity	81
orbit, to	to go around a planet	82
patrolman	a guard or policeman who checks that there are no problems	Wu18
phenomena	(plural of **phenomenon**); things that are observed	81
planet	large object in space that orbits the sun	83
RAF	the Royal Air Force; the British air force	Wu18
silicon	an element (Si)	83
solar system	the sun and the planets that move around it	80
spacecraft	a vehicle that travels in space	80
suggestible	if you are suggestible, people can influence you easily	81
telescope	an instrument for looking at the stars	81
tribe	an ethnic group	80
UFO	an Unidentified Flying Object; a mysterious object in the sky	80
vastness	immense size	83

weather balloon	a type of balloon that carries instruments to measure things such as humidity and wind	Wu18
witness	a person who sees something happen	Wu18

Extended reading 3   **See pages 84-85**

airlock	air trapped in a pipe	85
autobiography	the story of a person's life which they have written themselves	84
bog	an area of very wet land	85
bravery	being brave; courage	84
breed, to	to generate; to create	84
Cape Breton	an area of northeastern Canada	84
crippled	(here) very slow because of mechanical problems	84
cubicle	a very small, square building or room	85
flounder, to	to move around with difficulty	85
following wind	a wind that comes from behind	85
forced landing	if a plane makes a forced landing, it has to come down because of a problem	84
glide, to	to move through the air without using an engine	85
gull	a kind of sea bird	84
Hades	the ancient Greek name for the place where people go after they die	84
hut	a small building	85
innocence	the state of having no experience	85
limp along, to	to keep going with difficulty	85
motionless	not moving	85
muck	mud; dirt	85
mythology	myths and beliefs	85
Nova Scotia	an area of northeastern Canada	84
optimist	a person who is generally positive about things	84
pessimist	a person who is generally negative about things	84
propeller	blades that turn	84
seep, to	to move gradually	84
shatter, to	to break into small pieces	85
shipwreck	an accident in which a ship is destroyed	85
short-lived	which doesn't last a long time	85
shudder, to	to shake	85
snatch, to	to take hold of something suddenly	85
splutter, to	to make a coughing sound	85
stumble, to	to almost fall	85
submerge, to	to go underwater	85
swamp	an area of very wet land	85
trudge, to	to walk heavily or with difficulty	85
visibility	how well or not you can see, because of weather conditions	85